LAND OF PROMISE?

An Anglican exploration of Christian attitudes to the Holy Land, with special reference to *Christian Zionism*

*A report from the
Anglican Communion
Network for Inter Faith Concerns*

Published by The Anglican Consultative Council

First edition London 2012

Second edition London 2014, with amendments made by the 15th meeting of the Anglican Consultative Council, Auckland, 2012.

ISBN 978-0-9566596-4-4

© *The Anglican Consultative Council*

Set in Adobe Caslon Pro 12/ 13.8

Contents

Foreword

In his 2012 Easter Day sermon Archbishop Rowan Williams spoke of the 'intractable problems' of our time. He reflected: 'At Easter we cannot help but think about the land that Jesus knew and the city outside whose walls he was crucified. These last months have seen a phase of peace talks between Israel and the Palestinians yet again stalling, staggering and delivering little or nothing for those who most need signs of hope. Everything seems to be presented as a zero-sum game. And all who love both the Israeli and the Palestinian communities and long for their security will feel more desperate than ever… Listening to a rabbi talking about what it is like to witness the gathering up of body parts after a terrorist attack is something that can't be forgotten; neither is listening to a Palestinian whose parent or child has been killed in front of their eyes in a mortar bombing.'

The Archbishop went on to comment: 'So how do we respond? By turning up the volume of partisanship, by searching for new diplomatic initiatives, by pretending it isn't as bad as all that after all? If we believe in a God who acts, we have to go beyond this. We have to put immense energy into supporting those on the ground who show that they believe in a God who acts – those who continue… to bring together people from both sides and challenge them to discover empathy and mutual commitment… We have to prod and nag and encourage the religious leadership in the Holy Land on all sides to speak as if they believed in a God who acts, not only a God who endorses their version of reality. We have to pray, to pray for wisdom and strength and endurance for all who are hungry for peace and justice, pray that people will go on looking for a truly shared future. And we Christians in particular have to look for ways of practically supporting our brothers and sisters there… to help them stay in a context where they feel more and more unwelcome, yet where so many of them remain because they want to play a full part in creating this unimaginable shared future – because they believe in a God who acts. These are the priorities that all Christian leaders would want to flag up this Easter in our concern for what many call "the land of the Holy One".'[1]

This report, *Land of Promise?*, produced by the Network for Inter Faith Concerns of the Anglican Communion (NIFCON) and offered to the Anglican Consultative Council and to the Communion seeks to make a positive contribution in what is undoubtedly one of the most fraught and painful situations of our time. *Land of Promise?* has been written as a response to discussions about Israel and Palestine that have taken place at recent meetings of the Anglican Consultative Council, in particular the 14th meeting of the Anglican Consultative Council in May 2009 at which the issue of what is called 'Christian Zionism' was raised. Following on from that meeting, NIFCON then broached with the Communion's Standing Committee in December 2009 whether it would be helpful to provide a report on this topic to facilitate further discussion at the next meeting of the Anglican Consultative Council due to be held in November 2012. The Standing Committee warmly welcomed this proposal and *Land of Promise?* is now the end result.

In order to produce the report NIFCON appointed a small project group, drawing both from its own Management Group and from others who have a special interest in or understanding of the topic. The chair of the project group was Rt Revd Clive Handford, formerly Bishop President of the Episcopal Church of Jerusalem and the Middle East. Two residential meetings of the project group were held, and members of the project group also took opportunities to meet with those in Israel/Palestine, Europe and the United States known to have particular concerns or perspectives in relation to Christian Zionism. A preliminary draft of the report was then circulated to a wide-ranging group of individuals and organisations, including ecumenical partners, and representatives of other faith communities. Their comments were considered carefully and taken into account in the production of a final draft, which was presented to the Archbishop of Canterbury in September 2012. As the extract from Archbishop Rowan's Easter 2012 sermon quoted above makes clear, the Archbishop has himself a passionate concern for the areas this report touches upon and graciously agreed to write an Afterword for the report.

Land of Promise? is organised in eight chapters. It is prefaced by this Introduction which explains how the document was written. The report itself begins with a short reflection on the ambiguity of the term 'Israel' and the need to 'wrestle' with a number of difficult issues which touch on the heart of Christian identity. The second chapter seeks to clarify the terms 'Zionism' and 'Christian Zionism' as well as 'anti-Zionism' in a way that is accessible for a general readership, and briefly identifies some current key social and political concerns. In the third chapter we set out a number of statements and reflections offered by groups or individuals: this is done so that different, and sometimes conflicting, voices can be heard. The fourth chapter contains a number of real-life stories and incidents which are given as examples of the way the issues raised in the report impact on the lives of individuals, churches and communities. The fifth chapter presents a brief resume of particular features of Anglican theological method and Anglican theological resources for engagement with the topic. This is followed by chapter six, which surveys the history of Christian relations with the Holy Land and with Judaism, with particular attention given to the parts of this history in which Anglicans and the Anglican tradition have played a role. Drawing out the implications of what has been set out in the earlier chapters, in chapter seven the report offers a substantial exploration of three themes which between them take us to the heart of the issues under consideration: the gift of the land; exile and return; holy city and temple. The eighth chapter then presents a range of short conclusions, based upon what has been said earlier in the report. There is an *Afterword* offered by Archbishop Rowan Williams, in his role as Archbishop of Canterbury. It is intended that there will eventually be a study guide to accompany the report. The study guide will be structured round a series of Bible Studies.

Those working on *Land of Promise?* over the past two and a half years found themselves gradually wanting to widen the scope of their enquiry. As a result, although the specific phenomenon of Christian Zionism, and what might be appropriate Anglican responses to it, certainly remains a focus of the report, *Land of Promise?* also incorporates wider reflection on a number of linked issues. But various events, both political and religious, which have taken place during the period within which the report was being written have emphasised the pressures upon Christian communities in the Holy Land and the wider Middle East and the fragility of their ongoing presence. So the importance of 'Christian presence', linked so integrally to Christian belief in the incarnation, has become a thread which undergirds this report. Our participation in the Anglican Communion rightly means that we have a special care and concern for our Christian, and especially Anglican, brothers and sisters who live their Christian lives in the difficult circumstances of today's Holy Land.

Chapter 1

An encounter in the darkness

1.1   This report seeks to set out an Anglican response to the phenomenon of Christian Zionism, and to do so within a wider account of Christian thinking about Israel. The word 'Israel' has many meanings: it can refer to a people, a land, a state, an idea and so on. Rather than the object of a definition, though, Israel is for us first of all the subject of a story. In the Bible, that story begins when the name of Israel is revealed in a night-time combat with God. Jacob, about to cross the Jordan into Canaan, fears the hostility of Esau in the country of Edom. The night before he is to meet with his brother,

> Jacob was left alone; and a man wrestled with him until daybreak. When the man saw that he did not prevail against Jacob, he struck him on the hip socket; and Jacob's hip was put out of joint as he wrestled with him. Then he said, 'Let me go, for the day is breaking.' But Jacob said, 'I will not let you go, unless you bless me.' So he said to him, 'What is your name?' And he said, 'Jacob.' Then the man said, 'You shall no longer be called Jacob, but Israel, for you have striven with God and with humans, and have prevailed.' Then Jacob asked him, 'Please tell me your name.' But he said, 'Why is it that you ask my name?' And there he blessed him. So Jacob called the place Peniel, saying, 'For I have seen God face to face, and yet my life is preserved.' The sun rose upon him as he left Penuel, limping because of his hip. (Gen 32.24-31)

1.2   This mysterious passage has shaped the thinking and haunted the imagination of Jewish and Christian readers of the scriptures through the centuries, and is not without its ambiguities. The genealogical identity of Israel is defined as the patriarch and his sons the eleven, soon to be twelve, tribal ancestors; yet interpretative readings, both Jewish and Christian, resist pinning down its sense to any one meaning. Christian interpreters have seen in the Jacob of this episode a prefiguring of the Christ who will shape a new Israel; but they have also discerned here the image of the individual Christian who wrestles in the dark night of the soul with Jesus the 'traveller unknown'. The identity of Israel is confirmed before he enters Canaan to settle in it; yet this settler sees the territory as 'his own home and country', both the land of promise and the place of his birth and nurture. Jacob is in tension with his brother Esau, Israel with his neighbouring people Edom; yet when they meet their reconciliation is such that he declares: 'Truly to see your face is like seeing the face of God.' (Gen 33.10) The whole encounter is shot through with themes of anxiety, conflict and injury; yet it also becomes a scene of blessing, for central to its plot are both the hidden yet revealed figure of the divine wrestler and the threatening yet welcoming figure of the human brother: 'If Israel turns its back on either a relationship with God or a relationship with the foreign nations... then it becomes less than Israel'.[2]

1.3   So at the very start of the story of Israel we find woven together several themes we will have to address: the identity of the people called Israel; the experiences of belonging to, departing from, and settling in the land called Israel; the reality of conflict and the longing for reconciliation between Israel and its neighbours. We also find ourselves unavoidably challenged by questions about how we read the biblical text in the contexts in which we find ourselves – contexts which in many ways are shaped by earlier readings of those texts, and in many ways are also shaped by other forces, political, economic and cultural. And we have to recognise that, however much light we seek to cast on this story, there is much in it which will continue to be dark, conflicted and always beyond our comprehension. This is a story at the nexus of human history, drawing into its complexity, pain and confusion the aspirations and memories of people and peoples through the millennia; but it is also a story of the meeting of God with humanity, holding out to our world the prospect of divine blessing.

Chapter 2

Zionisms, anti-Zionisms, and the Holy Land

2.1   In our own time, it can often seem difficult to express any sense of a divine blessing being offered to humanity in and through the Holy Land. This is in part because of the evident and destructive conflicts and divisions which afflict the peoples of Israel and Palestine; but it is also in part because of the lack of an agreed language to describe both current realities and their historical background. In this chapter, therefore, before highlighting some of the problems facing the peoples of the Holy Land, we first discuss the various and contested meanings historically invested in the language of Zionism and in its opposite – anti-Zionism.

2.2   It is impossible to speak about attitudes to the Holy Land in modern times without engaging with the reality of the Jewish movement of Zionism; and it is increasingly necessary in speaking about Christian attitudes to the Holy Land to take account of the cluster of theologies and ideologies known as *Christian Zionism*. However, neither *Zionism* nor *Christian Zionism* has an agreed definition, as the following short selection of definitions and comments drawn from sources available on the internet show:

- Zionism is a form of nationalism of Jews and Jewish culture that supports a Jewish nation state in territory defined as the Land of Israel[3]

- If you believe that the Jews are a people, and support the right of the Jews to a national home, and you are willing to stand up for that right when it is challenged, then you can call yourself a Zionist, whether or not you belong to any organized Zionist group or accept any 'official' definition, and whether or not you live in Israel or plan to live in Israel – and whether or not you are Jewish[4]

- To many people in the West, most of whom fully support the existence of Israel *per se*, the term 'Zionism' has become a shorthand means of referring to those unwilling to relinquish Israel's rule over the territories[5]

- Judaism and Zionism are by no means the same. Indeed they are incompatible and irreconcilable: If one is a good Jew, one cannot be a Zionist; if one is a Zionist, one cannot be a good Jew[6]

- The Zionist Movement is a pure colonial movement that uses Judaism to serve its purposes[7]

- [Passover] should be a reminder of the essence of the Zionist revolution: the self-liberation of the Jewish People. Laid bare, that is all Zionism is. The notion that Zionism is somehow a colonialist, racist ideology is antithetical to its raw basis. Zionism was, is and always will be the emancipation of the Jewish People to be a free people in their own land[8]

- Christian Zionism is a belief among some Christians that the return of the Jews to the Holy Land, and the establishment of the State of Israel in 1948, is in accordance with Biblical prophecy[9]

- Christian Zionism is a movement within Protestant fundamentalism that understands the modern state of the country/region Israel as the fulfilment of Biblical prophecy and thus deserving of political, financial, and religious support[10]

- As Zionism is the belief in the Jewish people's right to return to their homeland, a Christian Zionist is by definition a Christian who supports the Jewish people's right to return to their homeland. Under this broad definition, many Christians qualify though their reasons for this support differ[11]

- If Christian Zionists are Christians in the sense that they believe Jesus is the messiah and the Bible the true Word of God, they are Zionists in the post-1967 sense because they also deny the Palestinians' right to be an independent homeland… Most Bible-believers and evangelicals and all fundamentalists are Christian Zionists[12]

2.3   Examples like the above could be multiplied almost indefinitely; what this small sample demonstrates is both that definitions of both Zionism and Christian Zionism are very diverse, and also that they are never politically, ideologically or theologically neutral. Evidently, the same must also be said of 'anti-Zionism'. The words we use always carry with them inbuilt assumptions, and if we fail to recognise this our conversations with one another will always be characterised by misunderstanding and suspicion. In what follows, we do not attempt to produce tight definitions of either term, but rather we seek to map some of the ways in which these centrally important but ambiguous terms have been used, and also to explore the relation between the two. Like anybody else involved in this contested area, we Anglicans bring with us our own assumptions; indeed, Anglicans of different backgrounds will bring different preconceptions with them. It may be that part of our distinctive vocation as Anglicans is to engage with one another in mutual challenge of those preconceptions, to enlarge our vision and sympathy as we learn from those whose views differ from ours.

a   What is (Jewish) Zionism?

2.4   In its most general sense, *Zionism* can be defined as the historic and continuing desire of the Jewish people for a homeland in the Middle East. In a narrower sense, it refers specifically to the movement of thought, literature and politics which from the later nineteenth century onwards has been committed to obtaining and securing such a homeland for the Jewish people, focusing (after some debate over alternative venues) on Palestine, and leading in 1948 to the declaration of the State of Israel.

2.5   It is important to remember that Zionism, in its first phase a predominantly secular phenomenon, was strongly opposed within nineteenth and early-twentieth-century Jewish communities in the West. Such opposition came both from traditional orthodoxy, according to which attempts to engineer a return from exile to Israel were a presumptuous usurpation by humans of a role reserved for God, and also from liberal assimilationism, which saw in the focus on an overseas homeland a dangerous distraction from the prime challenge of integration into modern societies. However, during the twentieth century there was a growing acceptance of the importance of Zionism for Jewish people, shaped by the dramatic history of their communities: notably, the growing insecurity of Jewish communities within Europe, culminating in the catastrophe of the Holocaust (*Shoah*), followed only a few years later by the establishment of the Israeli State and then the watershed moment of the Six Day War in 1967, which led in particular to Israeli control over the whole of Jerusalem. As a result, Zionism in some form is now seen as an important dimension of Jewish life by the great majority of Jewish people both in Israel and in the diaspora, and among both religious and secular Jews, although non- or anti-Zionist groups continue to exist, some with a high public profile. Thus, Zionism is no longer a phenomenon without religious significance: it is impossible now to speak of contemporary Judaism without recognising the centrality to it of Zionism in one form or another.

2.6   It would be a mistake, however, to view Zionism in the broad sense as only a modern phenomenon. Despite repeated instances of exile and suppression, there has been a continuity of Jewish community life in the Holy Land from biblical times onward, and throughout Jewish history some exiles have made the journey, as individuals or in groups, to settle there. Most importantly, the longing for the Holy Land, and particularly for Zion, is an important part of Jewish tradition, and draws on such deep-seated scriptural and theological themes as: the promise and gift of the land to the patriarchs and their descendants; the experience of exile and the prospect of return; and the exaltation of Jerusalem as the city chosen by God himself as the dwelling place of his name. These are themes which need to be addressed by Christians in any account they may give of Zionism.

2.7   Historic as well as contemporary Judaism, then, can be said to have a profoundly Zion-ward orientation; yet the ways in which that broadly Zionist dimension is received and expressed are very varied, and often contested, within the diversity of Jewish life. Four areas can be identified as raising particularly significant clusters of questions which generate passionate debate and disagreement.

2.8   First, there remains the historic theological question: how far is the establishment of the Jewish homeland in Israel to be brought about by divine intervention, and how far by human effort – and how clearly can a distinction be drawn between these two? This is no longer only a question of the basis for the return of exiles to the land of promise, but also, with the political existence of the State of Israel, a question of the theological significance, if any, of that state for Jewish people. While most religiously practising Jews see the Israeli polity as in some sense an expression of the divine will, there are others who disagree vehemently: not only the non-religious who wish to emphasise the secular nature of the state, but also some among the religious who maintain the traditional anti-Zionist stance (including groups living within Israel itself which refuse to ascribe to the state any religious legitimacy, while recognising its *de facto* existence). For those who do see a religious significance in the State of Israel there is the further question of whether its establishment and continuing life should be interpreted as signs of the beginning of a Messianic age.

2.9   Second, there are related questions about the current identity and vocation of Israel as a country. Does this nation meet the aspirations which Zionism invests in it as a homeland for Jewish people? This is a particularly challenging question given the diversity of those aspirations, ranging from the avowedly secular to the emphatically religious. Beyond that lies the still more challenging question: What does it mean to speak of Israel as a home for the Jewish people, or even as a 'Jewish state'? On what kind of Jewish practice or culture is the Zionist project built, and what space is to be accorded in the Israeli polity to those who are not Jews? Does Israel have a particular vocation, among the nations of the world or within the Middle East, to which it should be held to special account, or should it be judged on the same basis as any other nation? These can be particularly sharp questions for Jewish people in the diaspora, whose Zionism will instinctively incline them to support Israel: on what basis is that support offered, and on what basis should criticism be offered?

2.10 Third, these questions about Israel's place and role have a particular ethical significance and urgency in light of the situation of the Palestinian people. The old slogan of 'a land without people for a people without land' may have been powerful in its offer of security to the endangered Jewish communities of Europe, but of course the first half of that slogan did not at all reflect the actual situation of nineteenth- or twentieth-century Palestine, which was very much a land with a people. From the beginning, the Zionist project saw itself, and was seen by others, as an answer to the so-called 'Jewish question'; but in turn it has from the beginning been itself interrogated by the 'Palestinian question'. Given the resonance for Palestinians of themes like dispossession and exile, the hope of return, and the centrality of the holy city, are there Zionist resources which can help to answer this question; or is Zionism necessarily a story of Jewish exceptionalism?

2.11 Fourth, there are inescapably pressing political questions about the map of this land: the relationship between Israel and its neighbours; the future of the occupied territories in the West Bank and of Jewish settlements; and, centrally, the status of Jerusalem itself, the city which has given its name to Zionism.[13] These are of course issues of immediate concern to those who live in Israel, but they also have a significant impact on community and inter faith relations in societies around the world; within the Jewish community and the Zionist movement, a wide range of views will be found.

2.12 On all these questions Jews who would describe themselves as Zionists differ from and disagree with one another to such an extent that it may be more appropriate to speak of 'various Zionisms' than of one monolithic 'Zionism'. As we come to 'Christian Zionism' we shall find an equally complex and contested set of meaning and beliefs.

b   What is Christian Zionism?

2.13 Most Christians, including most Anglicans, would probably not define themselves as being either 'pro- or 'anti-Zionist'. There is a wide range of attitudes among Christians to Holy Land issues, reflecting some deep ambiguities in Christian faith over the theological significance of the Holy Land. Some will describe themselves, or be described by others, as Christian Zionists; yet Christian Zionism cannot be simply defined as Christian support for Jews in their Zionism, but rather refers to particular Christian ways of thinking and acting which issue in positions overlapping with some forms of Jewish Zionism. However, support for Zionism is much less firmly anchored in Christian theology than it is even in traditional Judaism; many Christians who are sympathetic to the Zionist project could not be described as Christian Zionists, but base their thinking on other, less theologically specific, grounds. On the other hand, Zionism itself, and still more Christian Zionism, are strongly repudiated by many Christians as inauthentic and erroneous. Conceptually, both Christian Zionism and Christian anti-Zionism, as they express attitudes to Jewish people as a group outside the community of Christian faith, are in a different category to Jewish Zionism, and they exercise a different theological function.

2.14 It is important first of all, then, to distinguish between narrower and broader senses of Christian Zionism – or, we might say, between Christian Zionism itself and Christian support for, or sympathy with, Jewish Zionism. In its narrow sense, Christian Zionism refers to a particular movement within evangelical Christianity, which dates from the nineteenth century, although with earlier roots in the Puritan period of the seventeenth century. Using certain key biblical texts it articulates, on the basis of its understanding of Christian faith, support for the continuing return or restoration of the Jewish diaspora to a homeland in the Middle East centred on Jerusalem. It also looks to an apocalyptic resolution of human history, and currently propounds an ideology of support for the State of Israel, finding practical expression in more or less uncritical support for Israeli positions in conflicts with Palestinian and Arab interests. In this narrower sense of the word, the political dimension of Christian Zionism is particularly emphasised by most contemporary scholars, one of whom has succinctly defined it as follows: 'Political action, informed by specifically Christian commitments, to promote or preserve Jewish control over the geographic area now containing Israel and the occupied Palestinian territories.'[14]

There are a variety of types of Christian Zionism in this narrower sense and particular biblical texts become especially important to specific groups. All would pay attention to the threefold promise of God to Abraham in Gen 12.2-3, which they would suggest is apparently being fulfilled in the establishment of the State of Israel. Most however could also be described as pre-millennialist, drawing on the apocalyptic vision of Rev 20.2, which describes a millennium or thousand-year period of Messianic rule, during which Satan is bound and his power restrained. Pre-millennialist Christian Zionists seek to draw (or even potentially instigate) connections between current realities in the Middle East and such apocalyptic events. In addition, the majority of pre-millenialist Christian Zionists have also adopted a set of distinctive theological principles and methods of biblical interpretation known as 'dispensationalism', which evolved in the latter part of the nineteenth century. Based on 2 Tim 2.15,[15] it attempts to divide history into a series of 'dispensations' or epochs.[16] Such pre-millennial dispensationalist forms of Christian Zionism, popularised by writers and preachers such as John Hagee, Hal Lindsey and Tim LaHaye, have become increasingly influential over the last two decades, particularly in evangelical circles in the United States: when the epithet *Christian Zionism* is used without further qualification it now most often refers to such beliefs.[17]

2.15   The broader sense of Christian Zionism, or Christian support for Zionism, refers to a generalised Christian appreciation of the importance of the continuing existence and security of Israel, and a commitment to honour that importance within the context of fostering positive Christian-Jewish relations. As some form of Zionism has become the mainstream position of worldwide Judaism, so the need for Christians to acknowledge the significance of Jewish attachment to the Land of Israel has become manifest in dialogue between Christians and Jews. The internationally significant statement by a group of Jewish scholars, *Dabru Emet* (2001), noted with satisfaction: 'Christians can respect the claims of the Jewish people upon the land of Israel... Many Christians support the State of Israel for reasons far more profound than mere politics. As Jews, we applaud this support'.[18]

2.16   Within this broad arena, the 'reasons far more profound than politics' mentioned by *Dabru Emet* as generating Christian support for Israel, and so for the Zionist project, will be very varied. For some Christians, the motive will be primarily dialogical: recognition of the importance of Zionism for Jews means that Christians need to take their Jewish partners' commitment to Israel with utmost seriousness. There may also be a strong sense, particularly within the continental European churches, of the need for Christians to defend Israel as a secure homeland for Jews in light of Christian complicity in the long history of anti-Judaism and antisemitism which culminated in the Holocaust. The terrible history of Christian anti-Judaism in Europe has been the cause of much reflection and this leads many to pray for the strength and wellbeing of the continuing Jewish presence in the Land. Many feel that the Church has a moral duty in this; others may suffer immense feelings of guilt.

2.17 Many Christians take a pragmatic approach towards Israel, which they believe to be in keeping with general Christian values and responsibility towards others. This might include accepting the existence of the State of Israel as a given, and even admiring the work undertaken by a relatively few generations of Israelis to build up its infrastructure. They would want to stress that Israel is a democracy and that, irrespective of any disagreements with the actions of its government, there are far worse things happening under other regimes. They would suggest that the critical attention focused on Israel's actions, and the calls for boycotts and sanctions, is in itself unjust. All these, and other, approaches may also be coupled with a desire to see the Jewish people prosper, as 'the first to hear God's word'.

2.18 Again, some would want to stress as Christians the significance of the State of Israel for Jews both in Israel and the diaspora, as the only national state within which the calendar of the year moves in tune with Hebrew festivals, where the language is Hebrew, and which could be regarded as a natural 'safe haven' in times of trouble elsewhere. While some from this approach have no specific interest in Palestinian Christians and Muslims, others are equally concerned for all people and their different needs.

2.19 Others will identify theological imperatives within their own Christian faith which motivate them to a pro-Zionist position. Besides the ideology of Christian Zionism as narrowly defined above, these may include a more general sense of the fulfilment of promises of return in the twentieth-century history of Israel, a prioritisation of the place of Jewish believers and of Jerusalem as central to the life of the Church, and a deep-seated attachment to the Holy Land as the scene of the Lord's earthly life which has led them to appreciate the Jewish roots of his ministry and teaching. All these factors can generate among Christians a Zion-ward orientation to their faith which, while rarely as passionate as that among Jews, is based on important theological principles, and which finds among those principles a basis for some degree of Christian support for the continuing Zionist project.

2.20 As with Jewish Zionists, so among Christian Zionists in this broad sense also there is a wide variety of views over such questions as the theological status of the land of Israel, the place of the State of Israel, the situation of the Palestinian people, the political realities of Israel's relations with its neighbours, the occupied territories and new settlements, and the status of Jerusalem. In addition, there is a particular cause of disagreement to be found among Christian Zionists which, not surprisingly, is not present among Jewish Zionists: namely, the question of the conversion of Jewish people to faith in Jesus as Messiah. For some who are strongly committed to support for Israel, this is a necessary expectation on the part of the Church, and therefore mission to Jewish people should be pursued alongside a Zionist political stance.[19] For others – particularly those who adopt the theological stance known as *dispensationalism* – the expectation is that, as part of the sequence of events which mark the end times, Jewish people should return to Israel without committing to belief in the Christ; an evangelising mission towards them is, on this view, not part of God's plan.

2.21   With all these ranges of theological and practical attitudes in mind, it is as appropriate to speak of a variety of *Christian Zionisms* as it is to recognise a variety of (Jewish) *Zionisms*. At the same time, we also need to keep in focus the particular historical movement and current ideology of the more narrowly defined dispensationalist model of Christian Zionism identified above. In current discourse – whether that of theological debate, political analysis or scholarly research – it is usually the latter which is being referred to when the expression *Christian Zionism* is used. In this report, we seek specifically to address Christian Zionism by articulating an Anglican response, which at the same time takes account of the variety of Christian positions on Holy Land issues, among them those broadly supportive of Zionism.

c   What is (Christian) anti-Zionism?

2.22   It is important, though, to remember that that wider Christian variety includes not only those who could be described as broadly *pro-Zionist* but also those who are definitely *anti-Zionist*. There are many Christians for whom an anti-Zionist stance is mandated by the realities of the current situation: the need for peace and justice in the Middle East, to which the Zionist project is seen to be hostile; the importance of adherence to international law; a particular concern for the indigenous churches of the Holy Land, whose significance seems to be disallowed by Christian Zionism; and, for some, the greater urgency of the dialogue with Islam. Some would hope for an end to the State of Israel and the establishment of a different government throughout the Holy Land. Their reasons may be based on a pragmatic or political train of thought, although some may see this as the only way to follow the prophetic injunction to 'do justly'.

2.23   Anti-Zionism among Christians may also be based on theological principles – most obviously, perhaps, the teaching commonly described as *supersessionism*, which holds that the Jewish people have been definitively replaced by the Church as the new Israel, so that Judaism and Israel AD no longer have the significance that they had BC. Such a view naturally lends itself to anti-Zionism, as it leaves no theological space for a continuing geographical or demographic Israel in the new covenant. Supersessionism in this sense cannot, however, be simply identified with the Church's traditional teaching, as this did in fact ascribe a continuing importance to the Jewish people in the Christian era. Nevertheless, that importance was seen in negative terms, as a continuing chastisement by God for their sin of disobedience; this in turn was obviously not a theological position which would lead to a sympathy with Zionism. Some Christians again may see the Jewish people as having forfeited any rights to the Land as a result of their collective disobedience in rejecting Jesus as Messiah. In fact, the Christian motivations leading to anti-Zionism are so diverse and contested, as are the forms in which it is expressed, that it may be better to speak of a variety of *Christian anti-Zionisms* rather than of a unitary *Christian anti-Zionism*.

2.24   Of course, Christians may recognise elements of these various ideas as reflected in their own views, which yet are not fully expressed or delimited by any one defined position. Many would want to acknowledge that, however difficult the history and current state of affairs, the State of Israel does now exist and function with seven million citizens, and would maintain that the religious and moral imperative is to encourage and assist just and fair dealings from its secular government, particularly in respect of the suffering of Palestinians.

2.25   The most obvious risk that arises from the diversity of these positions is a growing sense of polarisation, both within the Anglican Communion and more widely among Christians. A further risk is that of the encouragement offered to antisemitism and to Islamophobia. The belief that the State of Israel represents the forces of good in a cosmic battle against the evil of Islam leads conclusively to the latter, while views expressed about the nature and purpose of both Israeli and diaspora Jews can in turn lead easily to antisemitism. As Christians, we need always to examine our own language and actions, and to distance ourselves from anything that is seen as incompatible with Christ's teaching.

d   What current social and political concerns affect Christian approaches?

2.26   Bearing this in mind, we now set down what seem to us some of the key issues affecting Christians, Jews and Muslims, Israelis and Palestinians in the Holy Land in the early years of our century. We recognise that others might place their emphases differently, use language in different ways, or tell different narratives; all description and all analysis is necessarily selective and partial in that it relies on certain assumptions and operates from certain viewpoints.

2.27   The year 2000 was anticipated as one of celebration at the beginning of a new Christian millennium. The outbreak of the Second (*Al Aqsa*) Intifada[20] in October that year, however, resulted in increased violence and repressive security measures. Stone-throwing youths in Palestinian territories were met with direct fire from the Israel Defense Forces. Captured soldiers were lynched and suicide bombings by Palestinian terrorists in public places and on buses resulted in many deaths and horrific injuries.

2.28   Israel's main response to individual terrorist attacks has been to build a Separation Wall – in some places a high, thick wall, in others a fence – intended to prevent terrorists from entering Israeli territory. Israel also maintains its military occupation of the West Bank. The route of the barrier is highly controversial, taking up areas of Palestinian land, beyond internationally accepted demarcations (*The Green Line*), and involving the destruction of olive groves and land farmed by local families for centuries.[21] The restriction of Palestinian workers travelling to jobs in Israel has, together with these other measures, resulted in severe economic deprivation. Numerous[22] check-points operate where Palestinians have to endure long waits, refusals to travel and other humiliations. The settlements built for Israeli Jews in the West Bank are protected by Israeli security forces, which restrict Palestinian movements in and around neighbouring villages, and there are serious concerns about access to scarce water resources in the region. Reports of violence and retaliations on both sides are regular occurrences. There are possibilities of redress through the Israeli courts, and some claimants have achieved a degree of success there, but Palestinians generally do not have much faith in the Israeli legal system.[23]

2.29   Gaza is separated from the West Bank, with its inhabitants confined under siege conditions and its borders between Israel and Egypt heavily policed; only basic goods are allowed through, although an extensive tunnel network has been in use. Attempts to run the Israeli naval blockade by international groups of activists have been largely unsuccessful and the blockade remains in place. International humanitarian organisations have highlighted the crisis the siege is causing for Gazans.[24] Jewish Israeli settlements there were all disbanded by Ariel Sharon in 2006 in an operation which was difficult and controversial within Israel.

Gaza is controlled by Hamas. Despite its having been democratically elected,[25] most governments regard Hamas as a terrorist organisation, committed to the destruction of Israel, and do not therefore recognise its authority. Following the Palestinian elections, a rift developed between the Fatah-run Palestinian Authority in the West Bank and Gaza under Hamas control. Recently, there have been moves towards cooperation, culminating in the Doha Deal, but in practice cooperation remains difficult. Southern Israel is vulnerable to ongoing missile attacks launched from Gaza. In December 2008, Israel launched a heavy military offensive, widely condemned internationally as hugely disproportionate, resulting in considerable Palestinian loss of life.[26]

2.30   As a result of these events, and by mismanagement, the Palestinian standard of living is significantly lower than that of Israelis. Palestinians in the West Bank, Gaza and most of East Jerusalem are without passports. International travel documents have to be obtained through Jordan, and travel outside their localities involves applications for visas from the Israeli authorities which may or may not be granted and can be subject to cancellation. Residency permits are organised on a local basis; in practice this means that families divided between the Bethlehem area and East Jerusalem, a distance of only a few miles, are subject to travel restrictions, long delays at check-points and possible refusals. For Palestinians, both Christians and Muslims, all this has often meant that they have been unable to worship in Jerusalem at festival times or have been refused permission to travel to Al Aqsa. Furthermore, journeys to church for many Christians which used to take a few minutes can now take hours, or not be possible at all. While access to holy sites is accepted both by Israel and internationally as a right to be respected, in practice it may be restricted. Rachel's Tomb, near Bethlehem, is now totally inaccessible to all Christians. The mosque and cemetery on the site are also inaccessible to Muslims.

2.31   Around twenty percent of Israel's population are Arabs; although full Israeli citizens, their language, traditions and ethnicity are Arab and they are mostly Christian or Muslim, with a significant Druze population. Bedouin families, mostly living in the south, are subject to increasing hardship as grazing lands and access routes are removed or blocked. The situation of Arabs who are Israeli citizens but increasingly identify themselves as Palestinian is a particular cause for concern; statistics show that they receive less government funding and often feel marginalised. They may also be subject to institutional discrimination. Palestinians from the West Bank and Gaza who are married to Israeli citizens have residency permits which restrict their activities in various ways, such as the withholding of driving licenses. Conversely, Israeli Arabs often cite benefits of Israeli citizenship; Israel also operates a system of Sharia courts where an Islamic legal system deals with civil matters subject to State principles.

2.32   In Israeli cities such as Tel Aviv-Jaffa and in East Jerusalem, Israeli Arab citizens are often expected to prove ownership of their homes, even if these have been in the family for many generations. This leaves them vulnerable to land seizure. In Jaffa, many Israeli Arabs took on homes left by Palestinians who fled in 1948; they and their families have lived in them ever since, but unlike other Israeli citizens they have been granted only *protected tenancy* agreements by the Israeli Government. Technically, these remain classed as *absentee ownership* properties, and currently these are subject to a wave of eviction, appropriation or demolition orders.[27] The situation of those who are Palestinian but do not hold Israeli citizenship is more difficult still. Permission for Palestinian building and extending in places such as East Jerusalem is rarely granted and all unofficial or legally unproven work is subject to demolition. The Jerusalem municipality's planning and building policy is a cause for concern, as means of access between the West Bank and East Jerusalem are now severely restricted. Some areas of East Jerusalem have been settled by Jewish families helped by ideological groups whose aim is to encourage Palestinian residents to leave.[28] While a few in these areas are acquired through sales from Palestinians, most homes acquired by new Jewish residents have been seized for one reason or another and their families evicted. Also of concern is the method of archaeological excavation carried out by a right-wing organisation under and around Silwan, a Palestinian neighbourhood in East Jerusalem.

2.33   Israel suffers the continuing insecurity of knowing that there are those committed to its eradication. Israeli Jews have a collective memory of recurrent persecution; their safe haven often appears a fragile concept, in danger of imminent destruction. Currently, the nuclear programme developing in Iran is a source of particular concern, not just to Israel, although Iran has often called specifically for its eradication. Support for Israel is still strong in the USA, which acknowledges its democratic and Western-looking regime. There are also strong lobbies in the USA – both from the Jewish community and, significantly, from Christian groups. Support from Christian fringe groups expanded considerably following the destruction of the World Trade Centre in New York in 2001 when the Battle of Armageddon – in which Israel would have a crucial role to play – was considered imminent. However, the USA has also warned Israel with regard to its continued building of settlements.[29]

2.34   A significant number of Palestinians live in camps with schooling and health-care provided by the UN. Local taxes and levies also provide support. Palestinians now have a small measure of self-government, but only severely limited powers to change anything; former administrations have also squandered international goodwill through corruption. Palestinians waver between stoical endurance and despair.

2.35   Of considerable significance has been the 2009 document *Kairos Palestine*, the culmination of more than a year's work by senior Christian Palestinian figures and signed by the leaders of Christian communities and churches in the region. Taking its name from the Kairos initiative of South Africa in 1985, it called upon 'all the Christians and churches in the world asking them to stand against injustice and apartheid, urging them to work for a just peace in our region, calling on them to revisit theologies which justify crimes perpetrated against our people and the dispossession of the land'.[30] The document described the occupation by Israel as sinful, and resistance – but only the 'resistance of love' – as a Christian duty. The document further stressed a commitment to recognising the humanity of all and the sovereignty of God.

2.36   Since the early 1990s peace negotiations have presumed a two-state solution. This has been undermined by the building of new Israeli settlements on Palestinian land and the continuing hostility of Hamas and its extremist supporters in neighbouring countries. Problematic issues include the demand of Palestinians to return to their pre-1948 family homes and the needs of Israel to be secure. The question of Jerusalem is also difficult; demands made for Israel to relinquish ground captured in 1967 may include Judaism's holy site at the Western Wall and significant areas of the modern city. United Nations Resolution 242[31] has provided the basis for international law on these matters since 1967, but while laying down basic principles, it does not deal with any specifics.

2.37   In 2011, the Palestinian President Mahmoud Abbas submitted a request to the United

Nations for recognition of Palestinian statehood. There are many obstacles to achieving this, especially from international voices that prefer a negotiated peace as a first step solution, which seems currently unlikely. Many Christians have joined the calls for boycotts, divestment and sanctions in attempts to force Israel to address issues of Palestinian rights, although not all Christians agree that this is the best course (or even, some would say, necessary). A motion proposed in the General Synod of the Church of England in 2005 relating to ethical investment led to a crisis in Anglican-Jewish relations, thus underlining the differing perspectives and lack of apparent understanding between many Jews and Christians on these matters.

2.38   The continuing diminution of historic Middle Eastern Christian communities is a growing cause for concern. Christians are no longer the majority in the traditionally Christian towns, and for communities in some areas, such as Gaza, the future is uncertain. Paradoxically, Israel is the only country in the Middle East where the Christian population is officially growing; this is mainly due to the diverse nature of Christians – including those from Eastern Europe immigrating to Israel under the 'Law of Return', [32] from 'Messianic' congregations and also migrant workers from Asian countries.

2.39   The World Council of Churches set up the international Ecumenical Accompaniers Programme in Palestine and Israel (EAPPI) in 2003, both to support Palestinians and to report on the situation. In July 2012, a motion of support both for EAPPI and for peace and reconciliation organisations such as the Parents' Circle Families Forum was passed in the General Synod of the Church of England.[33] The debate and discussions around it led to tension between elements of the UK Jewish community and the Church of England, threatening to damage relations internationally.

2.40   In 2011, the Archbishop of Canterbury and the Roman Catholic Archbishop of Westminster jointly convened a conference at Lambeth Palace specifically on the Christian communities in the Holy Land, launching an initiative to raise practical support. Participants in the conference – Jews, Christians and Muslims from Israel, Palestine and the UK – were reminded by Archbishop Rowan Williams that Christianity is a 'strange, Middle Eastern religion' – not from Europe, America or the Far East. Christians have been called, he said, by God into a relationship with this place and with its history. Furthermore, he reminded the conference that we must talk of such things in a language of truth and love, in accordance with Christian values, and that the language of truthfulness should also be one that shows that we are grateful for the stranger.[34]

Chapter 3

Some statements and reflections

3.1   Given the complexity of the situation we cannot hope in this comparatively short report to reflect all possible perspectives. However we feel that it is important to allow voices of some of those closely and existentially concerned with the issues under discussion to be heard in their own words. The following statements and reflections offer a range of insights linked either to Zionism or to Christian Zionism. In each case the reason why the particular perspective has been chosen is suggested in a brief introduction. The statements and reflections are set out in broadly chronological order. As a conclusion to this chapter we set out a number of questions which we believe Anglicans reading these statements might wish to consider.

3.2   **Martin Buber: The Land and its Possessors**

Martin Buber was a Jewish philosopher, theologian, peace activist, mystic and Zionist leader. Born in Vienna in 1878, he moved to Palestine in the 1930s as the result of Nazi persecution. His exploration of the *I-Thou* relationship has been an immensely influential contribution to Christian as well as Jewish theology. Buber was a significant theological influence on a number of Christians who were pioneers in Jewish-Christian relations in the 1930s and 1940s, not least the Anglicans James Parkes and W.W.Simpson. Buber also exerted influence upon the Zionist movement, primarily through his writings. In 1939 Buber wrote an Open Letter to Mahatma Gandhi, who had questioned the validity of the Jewish claim to Palestine. The following is an extract from that Letter, *The Land and its Possessors*.

> A land which a sacred book describes to the children of that land is never merely in their hearts; a land can never become a mere symbol. It is in their hearts because it is in the world; it is a symbol because it is a reality. Zion is the prophetic image of a promise to mankind: but it would be a poor metaphor if Mount Zion did not actually exist. This land is called 'holy'; but it is not the holiness of an idea, it is the holiness of a piece of earth. That which is merely an idea and nothing more cannot become holy; but a piece of earth can become holy…
>
> Dispersion is bearable. It can even be purposeful if somewhere there is ingathering, a growing home centre, a piece of earth where one is in the midst of an ingathering and not in dispersion and from where the spirit of ingathering may work its way out to all the places of the dispersion. When there is this, there is also a striving, common life, the life of a community that dares to live today because it hopes to live tomorrow. But when this growing centre, this increasing process of ingathering is lacking, dispersion becomes dismemberment. On this criterion, the question of our Jewish destiny is indissolubly bound up with the possibility of ingathering, and this in Palestine.
>
> You ask, 'Why should they not, like other nations of the earth, make that country where they are born and where they earn their livelihood their home?' Because their destiny is different from that of all other nations of the earth. It is a destiny that in truth and justice should not be imposed

on any nation on earth. For their destiny is dispersion – not the dispersion of a fraction and the preservation of the main substance, as in the case of other nations. It is dispersion without the living heart and centre, and every nation has a right to demand the possession of a living heart. It is different, because a hundred adopted homes without one original and natural one render a nation sick and miserable. It is different, because, although the wellbeing and the achievement of the individual may flourish on stepmother soil, the nation as such must languish…

But this is not all. Because for us, for the Jews who think as I do, painfully urgent as it is, it is indeed not the decisive factor. You say, Mahatma Gandhi, that a sanction is 'sought in the Bible' to support the cry for a national home, which 'does not make much appeal to you'. No – this is not so. We do not open the Bible and seek sanction there. The opposite is true: the promises of return, of re-establishment, which have nourished the yearning hope of hundreds of generations, give those of today an elementary stimulus, recognised by few in its full meaning but effective also in the lives of many who do not believe in the message of the Bible. Still, this too is not the determining factor for us who, although we do not see divine revelation in every sentence of Holy Scriptures, yet trust in the spirit that inspired their speakers. What is decisive for us is not the promise of the Land – but the command, whose fulfilment is bound up with the land, with the existence of a free Jewish community in this country. For the Bible tells us – and our inmost knowledge testifies to it – that once, more than three thousand years ago, our entry into this land was in the consciousness of a mission from above to set up a just way of life through the generations of our people, such a way of life as can be realised not by individuals in the sphere of their private existence but only by a nation in the establishment of its society: communal ownership of the land, regularly recurrent levelling of social distinctions, guarantee of the independence of each individual, mutual help, a common Sabbath embracing serf and beast as beings with equal claim, a sabbatical year whereby, letting the soil rest, everybody is admitted to the free enjoyment of its fruits. These are not practical laws thought out by wise men; they are measures that the leaders of the nation, apparently themselves taken by surprise and overpowered, have found to be the set task and condition for taking possession of the land. No other nation has ever been faced at the beginning of its career with such a mission. Here is something that allows of no forgetting, and from which there is no release. At that time, we did not carry out what was imposed upon us. We went into exile with our task unperformed. But the command remained with us, and it has become more urgent than ever. We need our own soil in order to fulfil it. We need the freedom of ordering our own life. No attempt can be made on foreign soil and under foreign statute. The soil and the freedom for fulfilment may not be denied us. We are not covetous, Mahatma; our one desire is that at last we may obey.

Now, you may well ask whether I speak for the Jewish people when I say 'we'. I speak only for those who feel themselves entrusted with the mission of fulfilling the command of justice delivered to Israel of the Bible… [35]

3.3   **Naim Ateek: A Palestinian Christian Cry for Reconciliation**

The Anglican Canon Naim Ateek, a Palestinian Israeli citizen born in Beisan and exercising most of his ministry in Israel/Palestine, has, both through his writings, and his key role in the establishment of the organisation Sabeel (see 6.49) had a significant impact on Palestinian Christian thinking about Zionism and Christian Zionism. In 2004 Sabeel organised a conference under the title *Challenging Christian Zionism*. Ateek's summary of the core beliefs of Christian Zionism is set out in endnote 17. By and large, when Ateek and Sabeel use the term *Christian Zionism* they are referring to the narrower sense of Christian Zionism (as defined in 2.14 and 2.21), but on occasion they also use the term in a broader sense. The first substantial book written by Ateek, published in 1989, which became the impetus for the foundation of Sabeel, was *Justice and only Justice*. His second major book, *A Palestinian Christian Cry for Reconciliation*, appeared in 2007. The following extracts, which set out Ateek's view of the danger of misuse of the Bible, are taken from an article he wrote in 1992 and *A Palestinian Christian Cry for Reconciliation*:

> In Israel-Palestine today, the Bible is being quoted to given the primary claim over the land to Jews. In the mind of many religious Jews and fundamentalist Christians the solution to the conflict lies in Palestinian recognition that God has given the Jews the land of Palestine forever. Palestinians are asked to accept this as a basic truth... Palestinian Christians must tackle the land from a biblical perspective, not because I believe that the religious argument over the land is of the *bene esse* of the conflict, but because we are driven to it as a result of the religious-political abuse of biblical interpretation.[36]

> In the last chapter of *Theology of the Old Testament* scripture scholar Walter Brueggemann discusses what he terms 'Some Pervasive Issues'. One of these topics is Old Testament theology in relation to the New Testament and to the church. He writes that 'Old Testament theology has been characteristically a Christian enterprise', with its primary focus towards the New Testament. In Brueggemann's view, this has led Christians into a notorious supersessionism, 'whereby Jewish religious claims are overridden in the triumph of Christian claims'... Brueggemann holds that the Old Testament is polyphonic in its testimony and that it is a misinterpretation to present only, 'one single and exclusivist construal, namely, the New Testament Christological construal, thereby violating the quality of generative openness that marks the Old Testament text.' Brueggemann's words are provocative and allow for a stimulating discussion. In response, however, I maintain that as a Palestinian Christian I read the Old Testament through the lens of my Christian faith. It is a part of my religious heritage and my holy scriptures. It is integrally connected with the witness of the early church of the New Testament. What renders the Old Testament important for me is the presence of the New Testament. The Old Testament alone, without the incarnation and redemption, without its fulfilment in Jesus Christ, would be interesting reading about the history and heritage of the Jewish people but would lack personal religious significance for me.[37]

3.4   The Jerusalem Declaration on Christian Zionism

In 2006 the leaders of four of the Churches in Jerusalem signed a statement condemning Christian Zionism. One of the signatories was the then Anglican Bishop in Jerusalem. It is based on an earlier statement issued at the end of the 2004 Sabeel conference on Christian Zionism, referred to above. The full text of the declaration is given below:

> 'Blessed are the peacemakers for they shall be called the children of God.' (Matthew 5.9)
>
> Christian Zionism is a modern theological and political movement that embraces the most extreme ideological positions of Zionism, thereby becoming detrimental to a just peace within Palestine and Israel. The Christian Zionist programme provides a worldview where the Gospel is identified with the ideology of empire, colonialism and militarism. In its extreme form, it places an emphasis on apocalyptic events leading to the end of history rather than living Christ's love and justice today.
>
> We categorically reject Christian Zionist doctrines as false teaching that corrupts the biblical message of love, justice and reconciliation.
>
> We further reject the contemporary alliance of Christian Zionist leaders and organizations with elements in the governments of Israel and the United States that are presently imposing their unilateral pre-emptive borders and domination over Palestine. This inevitably leads to unending cycles of violence that undermine the security of all peoples of the Middle East and the rest of the world.
>
> We reject the teachings of Christian Zionism that facilitate and support these policies as they advance racial exclusivity and perpetual war rather than the gospel of universal love, redemption and reconciliation taught by Jesus Christ. Rather than condemn the world to the doom of Armageddon we call upon everyone to liberate themselves from the ideologies of militarism and occupation. Instead, let them pursue the healing of the nations!
>
> We call upon Christians in Churches on every continent to pray for the Palestinian and Israeli people, both of whom are suffering as victims of occupation and militarism. These discriminative actions are turning Palestine into impoverished ghettos surrounded by exclusive Israeli settlements. The establishment of the illegal settlements and the construction of the Separation Wall on confiscated Palestinian land undermines the viability of a Palestinian state as well as peace and security in the entire region.
>
> We call upon all Churches that remain silent, to break their silence and speak for reconciliation with justice in the Holy Land.
>
> Therefore, we commit ourselves to the following principles as an alternative way:
>
> We affirm that all people are created in the image of God. In turn they are called to honour the dignity of every human being and to respect their inalienable rights.

We affirm that Israelis and Palestinians are capable of living together within peace, justice and security.

We affirm that Palestinians are one people, both Muslim and Christian. We reject all attempts to subvert and fragment their unity.

We call upon all people to reject the narrow world view of Christian Zionism and other ideologies that privilege one people at the expense of others.

We are committed to non-violent resistance as the most effective means to end the illegal occupation in order to attain a just and lasting peace.

With urgency we warn that Christian Zionism and its alliances are justifying colonization, apartheid and empire-building.

God demands that justice be done. No enduring peace, security or reconciliation is possible without the foundation of justice. The demands of justice will not disappear. The struggle for justice must be pursued diligently and persistently but non-violently.

'What does the Lord require of you, to act justly, to love mercy, and to walk humbly with your God.' (Micah 6.8)

This is where we take our stand. We stand for justice. We can do no other. Justice alone guarantees a peace that will lead to reconciliation with a life of security and prosperity for all the peoples of our Land. By standing on the side of justice, we open ourselves to the work of peace – and working for peace makes us children of God.

'God was reconciling the world to himself in Christ, not counting men's sins against them. And he has committed to us the message of reconciliation.' (2 Cor 5.19)

His Beatitude Patriarch Michel Sabbah, Latin Patriarchate, Jerusalem

Archbishop Swerios Malki Mourad, Syrian Orthodox Patriarchate, Jerusalem

Bishop Riah Abu El-Assal,
Episcopal Church of Jerusalem and the Middle East

Bishop Munib Younan,
Evangelical Lutheran Church in Jordan and the Holy Land

August 22, 2006

3.5 Is CMJ Zionist?

The Church's Ministry Among the Jewish People (CMJ) has evolved out of the work of The London Society for Promoting Christianity among the Jews (see 6.15). Although supported by Christians from a variety of churches and denominations, CMJ has formal links to Anglican structures. From its early days it has worked for the restoration of the Jewish people, though this has not simply been understood in a territorial or political sense. There are now a number of international branches of CMJ – including one based in Israel itself.[38] The following statement was offered by CMJ UK in response to the often asked question *Is CMJ Zionist?* The numbering given to each paragraph in square brackets is the numbering used in the document itself:

> Many people have asked this question of CMJ. But Zionism is one of those words with a variety of meanings. So in order to answer this question, we must study the interpretation of 'Zionism'.
>
> **If Zionism means the following:**
>
> [1] Standing with the Jewish people, as critical friends, after almost 2,000 years of Christian Anti-Semitism (some of it within the Church of England).
>
> [2] Combating Anti-Semitism, including the unconscious variety which causes some people, in the name of justice, to be unjust in their criticism of Israel.
>
> [3] Thanking God that after all their suffering as the most persecuted people on the earth, culminating in the Holocaust, He has provided a safe homeland for the Jewish people.
>
> [4] Rejoicing in God's faithfulness to the Jewish people, preserving them as a people for His glory.
>
> [5] Believing the Church has not replaced or given up on the Jewish people.
>
> [6] Believing God still has a purpose for the Jewish People, namely to bring them to faith in Jesus as their Messiah.
>
> [7] Taking a critical approach to the many criticisms of Israel, to ascertain whether they are true or false and defending Israel, where appropriate.
>
> [8] Condemning Palestinian terrorism.
>
> **Then CMJ is pleased to be Zionist.**
>
> *However, if Zionism means:*
>
> [1] Ignoring the plight and rights of Palestinians and Israeli Arabs.
>
> [2] Believing the Palestinians and Israeli Arabs have no right to be in the Holy Land.
>
> [3] Believing Israel is above criticism and can do no wrong.
>
> [4] Ignoring the genuine examples of breaches of human rights and military over-reactions by Israel.
>
> [5] Ignoring the Biblical ethical demands, in terms of Israel's treatment of non-Jews, in that the Torah (Jewish Law) commands Jewish People to treat non-Jews as well as they treat fellow Jews.
>
> *Then CMJ is definitely not Zionist.*[39]

3.6   The Twelve Points of Berlin

In July 2009 the International Council of Christians and Jews (the umbrella body for national Councils of Christians and Jews, of which the relevant Anglican Churches are normally members) issued a statement at its annual meeting in Berlin. Called the Twelve Points of Berlin, it was seeking to update for the contemporary period the foundational document of the ICCJ, the Ten Points of Seelisberg, issued in 1947. The Twelve Points of Berlin has three sections. The first is addressed to Christians and Christian communities; the second to Jews and Jewish Communities; the third to both Jews and Christians, and others as well. The extract below sets out Point 4 (addressed to Christians) and Points 7 and 8 addressed to Jews:

A Call to Christians and Christian communities

Point 4: To pray for the peace of Jerusalem

- By promoting the belief in an inherent connectedness between Christians and Jews.

- By understanding more fully Judaism's deep attachment to the Land of Israel as a fundamental religious perspective and many Jewish people's connection with the State of Israel as a matter of physical and cultural survival.

- By reflecting on ways that the Bible's spiritual understanding of the land can be better incorporated into Christian faith perspectives.

- By critiquing the policies of Israeli and Palestinian governmental and social institutions when such criticism is morally warranted, at the same time acknowledging both communities' deep attachment to the land.

- By critiquing attacks on Zionism when they become expressions of antisemitism.

- By joining with Jewish, Christian and Muslim peace workers, with Israelis and Palestinians, to build trust and peace in a Middle East where all can live secure in independent, viable states rooted in international law and guaranteed human rights.

- By enhancing the security and prosperity of Christian communities both in Israel and Palestine.

- By working for improved relations among Jews, Christians and Muslims in the Middle East and the rest of the world.

A call to Jews and to Jewish communities

Point 7: To differentiate between fair-minded criticism of Israel and anti-Semitism

- By understanding and promoting biblical examples of just criticism as expressions of loyalty and love.

- By helping Christians appreciate that communal identity and inter-connectedness are intrinsic to Jewish self-understanding, in addition

21

to religious faith and practice, therefore making the commitment to the survival and security of the State of Israel of great importance to most Jews.

Point 8: To offer encouragement to the State of Israel as it works to fulfil the ideals stated in its founding documents, a task Israel shares with many nations of the world.

- By ensuring equal rights for religious and ethnic minorities, including Christians, living within the Jewish state.

- By achieving a just and peaceful resolution of the Israeli-Palestinian conflict.[40]

3.7   The Kairos Palestine Document

A Moment of Truth, more widely known as the *Kairos Palestine* document, deliberately reflecting the title of the Kairos document promulgated in South Africa in 1985, was issued in December 2009. The list of authors of the document contains at least two Palestinian Anglicans, including Canon Naim Ateek. It is endorsed by most of the Jerusalem Church leadership (though a distinction has been made between *signing* and *endorsement*). It does not explicitly refer to Christian Zionism, but responding to such ideology seems to underlie the document at various points. Quotations from *A Moment of Truth/Kairos Palestine* are given elsewhere in this report: here we give a longer extract from the document. The numbering given to each paragraph in square brackets is the numbering used in the document itself:

We believe in one God, a good and just God

[2.1] We believe in God, one God, Creator of the universe and of humanity. We believe in a good and just God, who loves each one of his creatures. We believe that every human being is created in God's image and likeness and that every one's dignity is derived from the dignity of the Almighty One. We believe that this dignity is one and the same in each and all of us. This means for us, here and now, in this land in particular, that God created us not so that we might engage in strife and conflict but rather that we might come and know and love one another, and together build up the land in love and mutual respect.

[2.1.1] We also believe in God's eternal Word, His only Son, our Lord Jesus Christ, whom God sent as the Saviour of the world.

[2.1.2] We believe in the Holy Spirit, who accompanies the Church and all humanity on its journey. It is the Spirit that helps us to understand Holy Scripture, both Old and New Testaments, showing their unity, here and now. The Spirit makes manifest the revelation of God to humanity, past, present and future.

How do we understand the word of God?

[2.2] We believe that God has spoken to humanity, here in our country:

'Long ago God spoke to our ancestors in many and various ways by the prophets, but in these last days God has spoken to us by a Son, whom God appointed heir of all things, through whom he also created the worlds' (Heb 1.1-2)

[2.2.1] We, Christian Palestinians, believe, like all Christians throughout the world, that Jesus Christ came in order to fulfil the Law and the Prophets. He is the Alpha and the Omega, the beginning and the end, and in his light and with the guidance of the Holy Spirit, we read the Holy Scriptures. We meditate upon and interpret Scripture just as Jesus Christ did with the two disciples on their way to Emmaus. As it is written in the Gospel according to Saint Luke: 'Then beginning with Moses and all the prophets, he interpreted to them the things about himself in all the scriptures' (Lk 24.27).

[2.2.2] Our Lord Jesus Christ came, proclaiming that the Kingdom of God was near. He provoked a revolution in the life and faith of all humanity. He came with 'a new teaching' (Mk 1.27), casting a new light on the Old Testament, on the themes that relate to our Christian faith and our daily lives, themes such as the promises, the election, the people of God and the land. We believe that the Word of God is a living Word, casting a particular light on each period of history, manifesting to Christian believers what God is saying to us here and now. For this reason, it is unacceptable to transform the Word of God into letters of stone that pervert the love of God and His providence in the life of both peoples and individuals. This is precisely the error in fundamentalist Biblical interpretation that brings us death and destruction when the word of God is petrified and transmitted from generation to generation as a dead letter. This dead letter is used as a weapon in our present history in order to deprive us of our rights in our own land.

Our land has a universal mission

[2.3] We believe that our land has a universal mission. In this universality, the meaning of the promises, of the land, of the election, of the people of God open up to include all of humanity, starting from all the peoples of this land. In light of the teachings of the Holy Bible, the promise of the land has never been a political programme, but rather the prelude to complete universal salvation. It was the initiation of the fulfilment of the Kingdom of God on earth.

[2.3.1] God sent the patriarchs, the prophets and the apostles to this land so that they might carry forth a universal mission to the world. Today we constitute three religions in this land, Judaism, Christianity and Islam. Our land is God's land, as is the case with all countries in the world. It is holy inasmuch as God is present in it, for God alone is holy and sanctifier. It is the duty of those of us who live here, to respect the will of God for this land. It is our duty to liberate it from the evil of injustice and war. It is God's land and therefore it must be a land of reconciliation, peace and love. This is indeed possible. God has put us here as two peoples, and God gives us the capacity, if we have the will, to live together and establish in it justice and peace, making it in reality God's land: '*The earth is the Lord's and all that is in it, the world, and those who live in it*' (Ps. 24.1).

[2.3.2] Our presence in this land, as Christian and Muslim Palestinians, is not accidental but rather deeply rooted in the history and geography of this land resonant with the connectedness of any other people to the land it lives in. It was an injustice when we were driven out. The West sought to make amends for what Jews had endured in the countries of Europe, but it made amends on our account and in our land. They tried to correct an injustice and the result was a new injustice.

[2.3.3] Furthermore, we know that certain theologians in the West try to attach a biblical and theological legitimacy to the infringement of our rights. Thus, the promises, according to their interpretation, have become a menace to our very existence. The 'good news' in the Gospel itself has become 'a harbinger of death' for us. We call on these theologians to deepen their reflection on the Word of God and to rectify their interpretations so that they might see in the Word of God a source of life for all peoples.

[2.3.4] Our connectedness to this land is a natural right. It is not an ideological or a theological question only. It is a matter of life and death. There are those who do not agree with us, even defining us as enemies only because we declare that we want to live as free people in our land. We suffer from the occupation of our land because we are Palestinians. And as Christian Palestinians we suffer from the wrong interpretation of some theologians. Faced with this, our task is to safeguard the Word of God as a source of life and not of death, so that 'the good news' remains what it is, 'good news' for us and for all. In face of those who use the Bible to threaten our existence as Christian and Muslim Palestinians, we renew our faith in God because we know that the word of God cannot be the source of our destruction.

[2.4] Therefore, we declare that any use of the Bible to legitimize or support political options and positions that are based upon injustice, imposed by one person on another, or by one people on another, transform religion into human ideology and strip the Word of God of its holiness, its universality and truth.

[2.5] We also declare that the Israeli occupation of Palestinian land is a sin against God and humanity because it deprives the Palestinians of their basic human rights, bestowed by God. It distorts the image of God in the Israeli who has become an occupier just as it distorts this image in the Palestinian living under occupation. We declare that any theology, seemingly based on the Bible or on faith or on history, that legitimizes the occupation, is far from Christian teachings, because it calls for violence and holy war in the name of God Almighty, subordinating God to temporary human interests, and distorting the divine image in the human beings living under both political and theological injustice.[41]

3.8 **David Rosen – Zionism: the perspective of a religious *peacenik***

In 2011 *Common Ground*, the journal of the London-based Council for Christians and Jews, published a special issue which focused on Zionism. Among the articles it contained was one entitled *Zionism: the perspective of a religious peacenik* by Rabbi David Rosen, founder of Rabbis for Human Rights. Rabbi Rosen has been a significant figure in Christian-Jewish dialogue over many years. He is a member of the Jewish delegation of the Anglican-Jewish Dialogue Commission, which has been meeting since 2007. The following is an extract from Rabbi Rosen's article:

> From a Jewish religious perspective, this ethical dimension is critical to the meaning and success of Zionism. The Torah not only declares that the Jewish people is ideally to dwell in the Land in order to live as a nation in accordance with the revealed Divine tenets and commandments, but that failure to do so undermines the ability of the People to live in the Land and leads to exile (Leviticus 26.27-33). Moreover this condition is overwhelmingly portrayed both in the Torah and in the Prophets in terms of the values of justice and righteousness and the social ethical precepts, especially towards the vulnerable and the 'other'. The Zionist movement sought from the beginning to achieve a *modus vivendi* both with the local Arab communities and with the Arab world. In 1919 the preeminent Arab leader, the Emir Faisal, co-signed a document with the president of the World Zionist Organization Dr Chaim Weizmann welcoming the Zionist enterprise and expressing the hope that Jews and Arabs would work together to bring about a flourishing of the region for the benefit of all. That dream was lost and conflict ensued with both Arab nationalism and nascent Palestinian nationalism. This conflict has caused much bloodshed, suffering, displacement and enmity. This should be a source of much distress to us who are proud to be called Jews and Zionists, for the vision of Torah and the vision of Zionism is one in which not only Jews but all people live in peace and dignity.

> The conflict has been costly for Israeli society. Generally, I believe that Israel can be proud of the fact that, despite the conflict, it has guaranteed equality of franchise and to a very large degree equality before the law for all citizens. However it would be disingenuous to deny that the conflict does impinge on the freedoms and opportunities of Israel's Arab citizens. While Israel assumed control of Gaza and areas of Judea and Samaria that constitute the West Bank as a result of a successful war of self defence in 1967, the price of controlling the lives of millions of Palestinians under occupation has inevitably had a deleterious effect on the moral fibre and institutions of Israeli life. That is why in my opinion a peaceful resolution of the conflict and the establishment of a Palestinian state alongside the State of Israel is essential not only for Israel's security, for the right of Palestinian national self-determination; but also for the health of Judaism, Zionism and Israel's moral character.

> For the same reasons I co-founded the organization Rabbis for Human Rights, because I believe that Jews who are true to their religio-ethical heritage are obliged to concern themselves with the human rights of others. If we disregard them in one place, that disregard will come back to haunt

us in another. This danger is patently obvious today to all who are not wilfully blind. [42]

3.9 **Questions**

- What do each of these statements or reflections *not* say? For example do statements from broadly pro-Palestinian voices explicitly affirm Israel's right to exist within internationally agreed boundaries? Do statements from a broadly pro-Israeli or pro-Jewish standpoint explicitly name Israel's current presence in the West Bank as 'occupation'?

- How do each of the statements or reflections use scripture? What are the factors which govern the choice of scriptural references and allusions in each of the documents? What is their theology of scripture? How selective is the use of scripture? Are documents from broadly pro-Palestinian standpoints adequate in their treatment of the Old Testament? Do documents from a broadly pro-Jewish standpoint allow adequate space, from a Christian perspective, for the role of Christ in relation to scripture?

- How do each of the statements or reflections understand the relationship between Christianity and Judaism?

- Some of the statements and reflections could be described as 'visionary' in their character. The current political and social realities in Israel/Palestine feel rather different. Does the difference between 'vision' and 'reality' invalidate such statements, or can it act as a prompt to work towards a transformed reality?

- What do each of the statements mean for the shape and health of Christian presence in the Holy Land?

Chapter 4

Some stories for Anglicans

4.1 We offer here a number of stories which show something of the variety of impacts of Christian Zionism in different parts of the Anglican Communion, and more generally raise issues about Christian attitudes to the Holy Land. While these are important themes in many contexts, they are clearly of immediate, existential and unavoidable importance to those who actually live in Israel and Palestine. The following story describes the experience of one Palestinian Christian told through the mouth of a Western friend:

> She was a middle-aged, middle class respectable Palestinian lady, a well-known poet and the wife of an Anglican priest, then living in Ramallah, a town just north of Jerusalem. One day, I met her gasping in disbelief from an encounter that she had just had with a Christian tourist from the West. On a visit to Jerusalem she had had a conversation with this person who, on discovering that she was a Christian living on the West Bank, had informed her quite categorically that 'she couldn't be a real Christian, because if she were a real Christian she would of course have been willing to leave her hometown, since she would know that God had given the land to the descendants of Abraham, Isaac and Jacob'. She was incredulous, and I was mortified for her, and angry on her behalf. The attitude she had encountered was one that many Christian Palestinians meet far too often.

4.2 The misuse of biblical texts to delegitimise the vocation of that Christian woman is quite clear in this instance, but the issues are not always so clear cut, as the following account shows:

> In 1975, at a time of major transition in the life of his diocese, the Anglican Bishop in Jerusalem proposed to draw up a lectionary for use in its churches. The group charged with this responsibility included a Palestinian clergyman working on the West Bank, a British expatriate responsible for the cathedral in Jerusalem and a Dutch minister who had been appointed by the previous Archbishop to liaise closely with the Jewish community. The discussions were lively! The Palestinian concern naturally enough centred on those sections of the Old Testament which majored on the conquest of the land at the time of Joshua; this felt in Palestinian eyes only too analogous to the events of the Six Days War, which had then taken place less than a decade previously. There was also antipathy to some of the New Testament canticles which normally form a regular part of Anglican worship. It is quite difficult to sing the canticle known as the *Benedictus*, beginning, 'Blessed be the Lord God of Israel who has visited and redeemed his people', and later referring to the Abrahamic covenant, if you are a Palestinian whose family has been dispossessed of land and home. Even the much cherished *Nunc Dimittis* feels uncomfortable when seen through Palestinian eyes – 'a light to lighten the Gentiles and the glory of your people Israel' provokes raw resonances. But there were also Jewish sensitivities to consider as well. There the concern centred on those parts of the New Testament, particularly in the Gospels of Matthew and John, where the hostility expressed to 'the Jews', especially at the time of Christ's trial and crucifixion, had been a terrible and diabolic justification

for the centuries of Christian antisemitism which culminated in the Holocaust. By the time that everybody's concerns had been addressed it was perhaps a miracle that there was much of the Bible left to read at all!

4.3   The impact of concerns relating to Israel/Palestine has also affected the development of Anglican liturgical texts in other parts of the world:

> 1989 saw the publication of a new Prayer Book by the Anglican Church in Aotearoa, New Zealand and Polynesia. Widely praised for its creative liturgical freshness, it also provoked controversy, particularly in relation to its translation of the psalms, called *Psalms for Worship*. A small number of psalms, or parts of them, were omitted on the grounds that they are 'not suitable for use in the corporate worship of the Church'. But the more controversial issue was the choice of the translators to downplay references to 'Zion' and 'Israel'. So, for example, the cry of Psalm 130.7, 'O Israel, hope in the Lord' now reads less colourfully, 'Wait in hope for the Lord', and Psalm 2.6 omits 'Zion' in the description of God's 'holy hill'. The changes clearly provoked debate. The Jewish community both in Aotearoa New Zealand and overseas saw the changes as an attempt to delegitimise the Jewish attachment to the land of Israel, along the lines of the attempts by some German Christians – allied with the National Socialist movement – to de-Judaize the faith earlier in the century, replacing expressions such as 'Israel' with phrases such as 'the people of God'. Members of the Prayer Book Revision Commission acknowledged that the references to Israel and Zion had been altered at the request of Palestinian Christians, who were concerned at the identification some people make between Zion in the scriptures and the contemporary state of Israel.

> The Auckland Council of Christians and Jews, commented that the changes to 'Israel' and 'Zion' were deeply offensive to Jews, not only for their political significance but because they suggested a cavalier attitude to scripture on the part of the compilers of *Psalms for Worship*. 'If people want to change scripture to make it "liturgically appropriate", as the Commission claims, they should write their own psalms.' An analogy was drawn to the use of Maori *taonga*. 'It's like taking a carving and painting it a different colour, because the old colour doesn't appeal today.' Aware of Anglican sensitivity to the feelings of Maori people, New Zealand Jews asked why the same sensitivity was not being shown to their spiritual treasures.

> Although the 1988 General Synod of the Church eventually voted to adopt *Psalms for Worship* it was significant that most Maori representatives either opposed the motion or abstained from voting. The Maori Archdeacon of Auckland said, 'He could culturally identify with the Jews and the transgressions of their cultural, historical and spiritual tongue'. [43]

4.4 The Israel/Palestine issue has also affected the development of international Anglican statements which explore relations with other faiths:

> The 1988 gathering was the first Lambeth Conference of Anglican Bishops to deal in any detail with the question of dialogue and engagement with other faiths and religions, at least in a positive way.[44] There was a considerable process of preparation for this, which led up towards the 1988 Conference. A draft statement had been produced. Because of the context of the members of the drafting team, who were based in the Western world, and particularly in the United States, it had focused primarily on relations with Judaism. But at the Lambeth Conference voices of Anglicans from, and having connections with, the Middle East argued that this was not adequate, and that the document also needed to engage more explicitly and positively with the question of Christian and Anglican relations with Islam. So at quite a late stage *The Way of Dialogue* (as it became) was altered from being a text which explored a bi-lateral relation with Judaism to one that looked at tri-lateral relationships between the three 'Abrahamic' faiths. A careful reader who subjects *The Way of Dialogue* to literary analysis can spot some of the rather creaking seams which resulted from this process. If the document had originally been designed from its inception to explore dialogue with both Judaism and Islam, it is likely that it would have been written rather differently. It is of course interesting to note that a similar process occurred in the writing of the Vatican II declaration Nostra Aetate: it too had originally been conceived as a text exploring Christian-Jewish relations, which had then been widened out to include the question of relations with Muslims, and with people of other faiths and beliefs.

4.5 Anglicans live among, and are affected by, the wider Christian community and climate in their countries in many respects, but not least regarding the issue of Israel/Palestine. Two examples are offered, one from Tanzania and the other from the United States:

> Elibariki Minja, a radio presenter on a Christian Radio station in Tanzania called WAPO Radio, believes Christians should support Israel as a nation due to the belief that Israel plays a special role in the eschatological future of the world. Elibariki Minja is the main presenter for a programme known as *Ijue Israeli* (Get To Know Israel). The following is a summary of the programmes broadcast in October 2010. *Ijue Israeli* does not have a distinct format, sometimes people who have gone to Israel come and share their experience, sometimes travel agents who organise trips to Israel use this programme to advertise their trips. A big portion of this programme serves as commentary to what is happening in Middle East and especially Israel. The commentary on Israel is mainly based on the Bible as understood by Futurist and Dispensational theologians. The comments are highly sympathetic to the Israelis and very negative towards the Arabs. Elibariki Minja calls himself *Muisraeli namba moja* (the number one Israeli). Minja's comments give the impression that what is happening in the Middle East is pre-ordained and human beings can do little to change anything. Trying to go against Israel is going against God himself and against his plans; since God is almighty no human being will succeed in going against God's plan.

In 1630 as his ship drew near the American coast, John Winthrop, the leader of a group of a thousand Puritans sailing to the New World, stirred his fellow pilgrims with the challenge to ensure that their new home was a virtuous example, a 'city set on a hill'. Nearly four centuries later, Gary Bauer, head of the Christian lobbying group American Values, and contender for the Republican Presidential nomination in 2000, drew on the same image as he promised that, 'A hundred years from now the star of David will still fly over Jerusalem and the Stars and Stripes over Washington – two shining cities upon a hill.' One of the reasons that Christian Zionist perspectives are so prevalent and popular in the United States is because of the implicit links drawn in popular culture between America's own past and Israel's present. The apocalyptic hope of the Puritan settlers in the early colonial period has become a taproot that is often drawn on by politicians when they speak of America's identity and vocation. But as with Bauer, some go further and make a comparison between the pioneer experience of America then and Israel now.

4.6   One final story reminds us how the conflict in Israel/Palestine can be transmuted into some strange keys, and impinge upon very different conflicts in other parts of the world.

Northern Ireland is a place of high emotional intensity, particularly where political affiliations are concerned. As often is the case with countries emerging from conflict, questions of identity are of paramount significance. One of the ways in which the struggles over identity express themselves is in the claiming of geographical territory by people of different groups. The flying of flags gives colourful expression to this. Transferred, or even second-hand, identities feature prominently, as might be expected in a globalized world. In parts of Northern Ireland, one will still find particular flags clustered in areas which are broadly either Republican or Loyalist in sympathy and in culture. A loyalist area will include flags of the Union of Great Britain and Northern Ireland (the Union Jack), which is red, white and blue; the so-called 'Ulster flag', which is predominantly red and white; the flag of Scotland, which is blue and white; the Glasgow Rangers football club flag, which is blue, white and red; the flag of the State of Israel which is blue and white. A republican area will include the tricolour of Ireland, which is green, white and orange; Glasgow Celtic football club, which has colours of green and white; the Palestinian flag which is green and white, and also of course black and red, which are less obviously relevant in the context.

Nationality, political affiliation and aspiration for a different political landscape combine with football to give voice to religious sectarianism and social exclusion. All of this gives colourful expression to an identity which presupposes deep-seated division and, in this case, draws the dilemma of Israel/Palestine right into the lived segregation of housing areas in contemporary Northern Ireland.

Chapter 5

Some theological resources for Anglicans

5.1   In an important sense, the theological resources available to Anglicans in thinking about the issues raised by Christian Zionism are no different to those available to other Christians, just as the history of Anglicanism in relation to the Holy Land is part of the wider history of Christian involvement there. In particular, Anglicans subscribe to the major positive changes in the theology of Christian-Jewish relations which have been received by the churches ecumenically over the last fifty years.

5.2   However, just as Anglicans historically have had their own particular narrative within the wider story, so there are some inflections within the ecumenical heritage of theology which are characteristically Anglican. Addressing the wider issue of an Anglican theology of inter faith relations, the report *Generous Love: The Truth of the Gospel and the Call to Dialogue*,[45] presented by the Network for Inter Faith Concern to the 2008 Lambeth Conference, identified a number of these, and we recapitulate them here, together with other motifs drawn from Anglican thinking.

5.3   *Generous Love* points out that the contributions which Anglicans make to the complex and contested world of religious plurality are shaped by the Anglican Communion's response to the Christian plurality of the post-Reformation world, developing the 'contours of a Trinitarian approach':

> Acknowledging that there is one God, the Creator, an Anglican approach dismisses nothing as outside God's concern, but attends to the world in its manifold differences in the expectation that it ultimately coheres, having one source and one goal in God.
>
> Acknowledging that God is manifest in the particular human life of the Son, Anglicans have been committed to working out their concerns historically... It [the Anglican Church] has treated with caution generalised claims made for timeless and ahistorical systems, preferring to make its judgements – including those relating to other religions – through seeking to discern the implications of the catholic faith within particular historical and social situations.
>
> Acknowledging that the work of the Holy Spirit is not just about 'inwardness' but provides the operative conditions for flourishing social life... Anglicans have been determined to minister to whole communities, to find ways of enabling people of robustly differing convictions to live together so that a public good may be formed. This understanding of the Spirit as the source of ground rules for productive social life is transferable to new situations of religious plurality.

5.4   These three principles of comprehensiveness, specificity and sociality, while they arise from the particular context of sixteenth- and seventeenth- century England, are recognisable as continuing instinctive characteristics of Anglican Christianity in very different historical and geographical situations; we shall see their relevance in particular to the Anglican presence in Jerusalem.

5.5   When Anglicans have sought consciously to identify their theological method, one theme which they have stressed has been the issue of biblical interpretation. We have not been able in this report to enter into detailed exegesis of particular passages, but we have valued the interlocking of scripture, tradition and reason of the threefold interpretative method which *Generous Love* summarises thus:

> The Bible has primacy in Anglican theological method, in that we seek to be a community living in obedience to Jesus Christ, the eternal Word of God who is revealed through the words of Holy Scripture. In identifying the message of the Bible for the present, the Anglican method brings the insights of tradition and reason to the interpretation of the text in the light of experience.
>
> Anglicans hold that Scripture is to be interpreted in the light of tradition and reason, meaning by these an appeal respectively to the mind of the Church as that develops and to the mind of the cultures in which the Church participates.

5.6   An important instance of the way in which tradition and reason shape our exegesis of scripture is to be seen in the interpretation of scripture, a matter of great moment for the particular subject we are addressing here. Anglicans will typically be suspicious of readings of prophetic texts which claim that their meaning can be simply and clearly read off from the page of the Bible without reference to the history of interpretation, to ethical or pragmatic considerations arising from the present situation, or to the experience of the living Christian communities of today.[46] Prophecy is understood as an insight into and a declaration of God's purposes for his people, a divine challenge to be met afresh as the people of God read the signs of their own times. Furthermore, given the importance of the Gospel of John for Anglican biblical study, theology and spirituality,[47] the stated purpose of this Gospel, 'that you may have life' (John 10.10; 20.31) acts as a key hermeneutical principle for Anglicans, a starting point from which we would wish to interpret scripture as a whole. From this basis death-dealing theologies which concentrate on cataclysmic war must surely be called into question.

5.7   The themes we are addressing clearly cannot be separated in the situation of Israel-Palestine from wider inter faith issues – in the first place, Christian-Jewish relations, but also the relationship between Jews and Muslims on the one hand, and between Christians and Muslims on the other hand. *Generous Love* sets out three dynamic patterns through which it maintains that churches can be renewed in their life and mission through encounter with other faith communities:

> First, maintaining our presence among communities of other faiths, we are abiding as signs of the body of Christ in each place. Second, engaging our energies with other groups for the transformation of society, we are being sent in the power of the Spirit into each situation. Third, offering... hospitality to our neighbours, we are both giving and receiving the blessing of God our Father.

5.8   We have found these three motifs of presence, engagement and hospitality helpful in thinking about what it means to sustain Christian life in the Holy Land alongside the life of other communities, and in exploring what might be meant by speaking of God's 'gift of the land' to his people.

5.9   Running through these ideas from *Generous Love* is an emphasis which Anglicans have always placed on discerning the grace of God present and working in the realities of human experience – in the histories people live, in the geographies they inhabit. This is for us a truth grounded on our faith in the Incarnation, God's living out of his life within the times and spaces of human life. The fact that the Incarnation took place in the Holy Land gives to the geography and history of this country an importance which no other land can have, but in approaching that Anglicans bring into play wider theological principles: a commitment to the discernment of God's action in history, a sense of the importance of place, and a recognition of the centrality to our faith of the sacramental principle.

5.10   The emergence of the post-Reformation Anglican settlement was conditioned by the complexities of sixteenth- and seventeenth- century British politics, and the missionary growth of the Anglican Communion was in many cases linked to British colonial and imperial enterprises. These linkages are particularly important, and particularly complicated, in relation to the history of Palestine and the Zionist movement. Anglicans cannot speak with credibility about the situation in Israel/Palestine unless they recognise how deep, how contested, and how ambiguous is the history of involvement which implicates us here. This historical rooting may sometimes be experienced as a burden; but it can also provide a schooling in the need to listen attentively and respectfully to the narrative of every community. Given this enmeshment of our churches in wider political and social stories, it is important for Anglicans to develop principles for discerning God's action in ways which do justice to the ambiguities of history. We shall see that a key influence and resource here is the account of providence developed by St Augustine of Hippo.

5.11   Anglicanism has also maintained a strong sense of the importance of place. This can be seen, for example, in the continuity of the parish system, with its principle of spiritual care offered to the people of a whole community; in the Benedictine inheritance of Anglicanism, with its commitment to *stabilitas*, sustaining divine worship in one place; and in the readiness to serve God in the first place within the particular duties of one's own local context, one's station. Particular places are of primary theological significance for Anglicans; none are more so than the Holy Land as a whole, and, within the Holy Land, Bethlehem, Nazareth, and above all Jerusalem.

5.12   Human space and time intersect with God's infinity and eternity in the sacramental. In the strict sense, Anglicans understand this as an 'outward and visible sign of an inward and spiritual grace given unto us, ordained by Christ himself, as a means whereby we receive the same, and a pledge to assure us thereof'.[48] They have refrained from defining the mode of this too closely as, according to historic Anglican formularies, that 'overthroweth the nature of a sacrament'.[49] More widely, the sacramental principle of a 'sign, instrument and pledge' in which meet material and spiritual, particular and universal, points to the mysterious yet real site of divine-human exchange we recognise in the Holy Land and the Holy City.

Chapter 6

Some history

6.1 The current situation in the Holy Land, and the current range of Anglican and wider Christian attitudes to it, can of course be understood only if we have some grasp of the historical background. Yet the historical material relating to Israel/Palestine is vast, complex and conflicted, and very differently narrated and interpreted by different groups and individuals. In what follows, we do not pretend to provide a comprehensive historical framework, but rather to focus on three themes: the persistence of Christian presence in the Holy Land and of Christian witness to its significance; the development of Christian Zionism as an identifiable strand of Christian thought and action; and the evolution of the current Israel/Palestine situation with particular reference to Britain's historical role. These themes are overlapping and intertwining rather than neatly separable, and we shall accordingly essay a broadly chronological rather than a thematic treatment; but throughout we will note in particular the ways in which Anglican Christians, and their precursors in English Christianity, have been implicated in the story.

a Early Christian and medieval periods

6.2 The Apostolic Christian community emerged in Jerusalem around the year 30 AD and first comprised Jews and proselytes from the Galilee region, Judea and across the Roman Empire. According to the account in Acts 2, those present at the first Pentecost included pilgrims from many parts of the Diaspora, including visitors from Rome and Arabia, as well as Judaeans. The first Christians were Jews familiar with a form of Judaism which was largely biblical, but influenced by the proto-Rabbinic approaches of the time.

6.3 As Christianity grew and developed in the Gentile world, the community in Jerusalem retained its significant position, despite being gradually diminished. After the destruction of the city by the Romans in 70 AD, little is known about the Christian church there for several centuries although there is a tradition that there was an unbroken presence of believers. In 135 AD, the Emperor Hadrian launched his building programme to remodel Jerusalem as Aelia Capitolina. Places of apparent religious significance were systematically obliterated and replaced with pagan temples, although Christian pilgrimage to Jerusalem and baptisms in the River Jordan were common as early as the end of the second century. When, in the fourth century, Christianity became officially accepted by the Empire, Empress Helena, mother of Constantine, attempted to locate sites associated with the life of Christ. Local Christian traditions directed her in this search, most famously to the suggested site of Golgotha, today enclosed within the Church of the Holy Sepulchre.

6.4 Apart from initiating a building programme to mark and honour numerous places of special significance, Constantine and his mother actively encouraged Christian pilgrimage. The focus of such pilgrimage was always the Christian interpretation of biblical sites, from both the Old and New Testaments. Scholars have pointed out that within this period, the fate of the Jewish buildings was intended to be instructive; the splendour of the Basilica of the Anastasis (the Church of the Holy Sepulchre) was to be seen in contrast to the desolate Temple Mount left barren as a sign of God's displeasure.

6.5 Christian scholarship and the religious life began to flourish in the Holy Land. One notable example was St Jerome who, in addition to his work on the Bible, led a monastic community in Bethlehem. He described the pilgrimage of a religious sister, Paula, to the region in 386AD, and his account is useful for outlining the sites of significance for Christians at that time. Jerome also gave considerable thought to the matter of Jewish conversion to Christianity and the relationship between Judaism and Christianity. In his desire to learn the classical Hebrew of the Old Testament in all its nuances, he associated with a number of Jews of different backgrounds, which drew condemnation from others in the Church.

6.6   Throughout the Byzantine period, the city of Jerusalem, now called Aelia, began to grow both in size and population, which was cosmopolitan. In 636 AD, the military conflict between the Byzantine Empire and the Muslim Rashidun Caliphate led to a six-month siege of Jerusalem and the subsequent arrival at the city of Caliph Umar to accept the surrender from the Patriarch. There are a number of stories about the period of religious tolerance for both Christians and Jews instituted by Umar. At the end of the seventh century, the Muslims began the construction on the Temple Mount of both the Dome of the Rock and al-Masjid al-Aqsa – the 'furthest mosque' as described in the Qur'an and visited by the prophet Muhammad on his night journey. It is also important to note that Jerusalem (*al Quds*) was the original *qibla* – the direction of Muslim prayer.

6.7   One major contribution to the literature of this period was made by the Venerable Bede, the English chronicler, in the early eighth century. His work *De Locis Sanctis* was based on the description of Arculf, Bishop of Gaul, who made a pilgrimage to Jerusalem sometime earlier. Falling victim to a storm on his return journey, Arculf landed at Iona where he described his travels in some detail to the Abbot Adamnan. Adamnan used Arculf's descriptions to write a guide book, complete with drawings and plans, also titled *De Locis Sanctis*, which described some of the major churches in the Holy Land. These included those at Jacob's Well, near Nablus, the Church of the Ascension, Mount Zion and the Holy Sepulchre. Bede later abridged this, together with the ground plans, to produce his work of the same name. It became a very significant source for scholars and pilgrims.

6.8   An early, positive example of Christian-Jewish dialogue in an English context was *Disputatio Iudei et Christiani*, dated as prior to 1098. In this Gilbert Crispin, Abbot of Westminster, recorded his theological conversation with a Jewish business partner.

6.9   The Crusader period continues to cast an ugly shadow on both Christian-Muslim and Christian-Jewish relations. In 1095 Pope Urban II called upon Frankish knights to lead a campaign to both 'free Christians from Islamic rule' and recover the Church of the Holy Sepulchre from Muslim hands. This was a violent and bloody period; Jerusalem was captured in 1099 and Western fortresses and infrastructure were set up throughout the Holy Land, guaranteeing Christian access to the holy sites. During this period, Christian pilgrimage and residency was encouraged. In 1187, the Holy Land passed to the hands of Salah ad-Din and his Ayyubid dynasty. Latin clerics and orders were forced or encouraged to leave, sometimes replaced by eastern Orthodox communities. After a period of conflict between various forces, control of the region subsequently passed to the Mamluks in 1260. In 1516 the Ottoman Empire seized Greater Syria, with Safed, Nablus, Jerusalem and Gaza named as distinct administrative areas within this region by the mid-sixteenth century.

6.10   Medieval life and theology had posed considerable threats to the Jewish population of Europe. Living in diaspora communities, Jews were outsiders and regularly blamed for everything from local murders and crop failure to the plague. Often regarded as being in league with the Devil, their continuing existence was a mystery to many, a reminder of the unfathomable eschatological purposes of God. Barred from most professions, they were tolerated and exploited as potential dealers in financial transactions and as money-lenders – something rarely open to Christians.

b   Reformed Anglicans and restored Jews

6.11   In 1290, King Edward I carried out the first of the Jewish expulsions in Europe, ordering all Jews to leave England. Although some Jews subsequently lived in England, it was widely believed thereafter that there was a continuing ban on Jewish residency in Britain. In the seventeenth century, expulsions from Spain and then Portugal sent waves of displaced Jews both to Palestine and to northern Europe. Life remained precarious. A distinguished Sephardi Amsterdam scholar, Manasseh ben Israel, was encouraged to propose in 1655 the opening up of England as a country of refuge for Jewish immigrants.

6.12   The guiding principles of the Commonwealth period were a major factor in Manasseh's decision to petition Cromwell. Puritan biblical hermeneutics in the early seventeenth century had developed an explicitly apocalyptic and Judeo-centric (though emphatically not philo-semitic) approach to the Scriptures. Focusing on interpretations of the Book of Revelation, this had proved repugnant to high church Anglicans such as Archbishop William Laud, who saw all too clearly its implications for monarchy. Conversely, the post-Regicide government set itself deliberately to adopt what it saw as a biblical line, and Jews such as Manasseh saw this as favourable to their interests. The Commonwealth government had invoked the prophet Amos in removing the seat of royalist legislature, the Star Chamber, and had referred to the story of Naboth's Vineyard in its cancelling of taxes seen as unjust. Another factor was the widespread belief that the Second Coming was imminent; passages in both Deuteronomy and Daniel suggested that Jews needed to be scattered throughout the earth, which included Britain. Manasseh set out the millenarian argument in two works, which were translated into English.

6.13   At the same time, the intersection of theology with politics cannot be underestimated in this early Jewish appeal to a broadly *Christian Zionist* (more properly *restorationist*[50]) way of thinking. Manasseh was not so much trying to persuade Christians to adopt a particular theological world view as he was seeking from them support for the political outcomes of that world view. In the same way, a few years earlier, one of the first identifiable political actions informed by 'restorationism' can be seen to be the petition made, from Amsterdam, in 1649 to Thomas Fairfax's War Council by Joanna and Ebenezer Cartwright. They requested the opening of England to Jewish inhabitation as a prelude to English co-operation with the Netherlands over transporting the Jews to the Holy Land.

6.14   In fact, there were undoubtedly practical, economic reasons for the English government to look favourably on the restoration of the Jewish community, as Jewish trading links and bases in Europe and beyond were valuable commodities. Although no formal declaration was made by the Cromwellian government, Manasseh and others were able to establish a thriving Sephardi community in England. By the early nineteenth century, the Age of Enlightenment, followed by the Age of Emancipation, had resulted in a largely pragmatic relationship between Jews and Christians in much of Western Europe. This was illustrated by the baptism and political career of Benjamin Disraeli, who became British Prime Minister, and by the affection and admiration of members of the Establishment towards others such as the philanthropic Rothschild family.

6.15   The London Society for Promoting Christianity among the Jews had been set up by a group of wealthy evangelical Anglican friends referred to collectively as the Clapham Sect and whose most prominent member was William Wilberforce.[51] The Society had its own distinct agenda, which involved declaring the Messiahship of Jesus to both Jew and Gentile, teaching the Church about its Jewish roots, promoting Jewish emigration to Palestine and encouraging new converts from Judaism. In 1811 it purchased land in East London to further its work among the Jewish community there.

6.16   In the 1840s, the London Society founded Christ Church, in Jerusalem, under the direction of Hans Nicolajsen, a Danish missionary. He was sent to Palestine specifically to further the aims of the Society – to share the Good News of Jesus Christ – and in anticipation of the return of Jews to the Land in large numbers, in what the Society understood to be fulfilment of biblical prophecy.

6.17   Around this time, a series of conferences took place in both England and Ireland on the subject of *unfulfilled prophecy*. In particular, these highlighted apparent promises of Israel's restored glory in the prophetic books. Previously these passages had been dealt with by, for example, seeing the prophecies as fulfilled spiritually through the coming of Christ. However, an evangelical Irish Anglican clergyman, John Nelson Darby, was among those who insisted on a literal biblical interpretation. He held that salvation history spanned a number of periods of time or *dispensations*, each of which involved God's dealings with humanity in a new or different way. The final dispensation would be inaugurated by the return of Christ to earth to gather believers into heaven ('the Rapture') before his millennial reign. For this reason, Darby's approach is described as 'premillennial-dispensationalism'.

6.18   Dispensationalism supposed a final glorious period in which both Jew and Gentile would recognise the kingship of Christ.[52] Darby's dilemma was how to explain the process for Jews of this recognition. He concluded that the present dispensation was *in parenthesis*, undergoing an interruption; in due course Christ would return once to the Gentiles, and a second time to complete the dispensation to Israel. Such thinking was influential in evangelical circles and helped to focus attention on Jews and Palestine as having major roles to play in Christian salvation history.

6.19   These developments in theology accompanied real interest in the region. After the capture of Jerusalem by Mohammad Ali of Egypt in 1831, earlier proposals from the Church Missionary Society (CMS)[53] to establish an official presence there progressed. The first Bishop, Michael Solomon Alexander, a rabbi converted to Christianity through the London Society, arrived from England in 1841. The bishopric was initially conceived as a joint Anglo-Prussian scheme, encompassing both Anglicans and Lutherans, with Christ Church as the first Anglican establishment. The focus of its work was the Jewish population of the area.

6.20   In the 1830s, the British Foreign Secretary Lord Palmerston supported a number of measures to help Jews abroad. His father-in-law, Lord Shaftesbury, was a fervent believer that the return of Jews to the Holy Land would hasten the Second Coming. Palmerston also worked to put pressure on the Ottoman Turks to allow Jews from Europe to travel to Palestine, arguing that European Jews, especially backed by Rothschild money, would be an asset to Turkish interests in the region. Lord Shaftesbury described Palmerston as 'an instrument of God in his dealings with His people', and likened him to the biblical Cyrus. In 1838 Palmerston appointed W.T. Young as the first western Vice Consul in

Jerusalem, with the remit especially to protect Jews. Between 1830 and 1850, contemporary reports [54] cited the rapid growth of the population of Jerusalem, mostly due to Jewish immigration.

6.21   Although not all British politicians were of the same mind, there was considerable sympathy for this approach. A number of philanthropic Jewish figures were also influential at this time, among them the President of the Board of Deputies of British Jews, Sir Moses Montefiore. A friend of Queen Victoria, he was also active on behalf of Jewish communities facing hardship or worse in both Europe and the Middle East. The British Prime Minister Benjamin Disraeli, despite his baptism and apparent assimilation, remained proud of his Jewish heritage, describing himself as 'the missing page between the Old Testament and the New'. He also took a keen interest in events of the Middle East, following a visit to the Holy Land in 1830.

6.22   Bishop Alexander was succeeded in Jerusalem in 1846 by Samuel Gobat. Noting the lack of success of the mission to the Jews, Bishop Gobat turned his attention towards Eastern and Palestinian Christians. In the 1850s a number of schools were built, including those in Jerusalem, Nablus, Ramla and Beit Jala, through the agency of CMS. Over the ensuing decades churches were established, including St Andrew's in Ramallah and Christ Church in Nazareth.

6.23   Following the lapsing of the Anglo-Prussian agreement, the bishopric became solely Anglican in 1887. The different missionary organisations retained their unique foci: the London Society remained based in Christ Church, Jerusalem and was primarily directed towards Jews. CMS remained deeply rooted in education and worked at developing the Arab Christian congregations. In addition, the Jerusalem and East Mission, founded by Bishop Blyth in 1889 was controlled directly by the Church of England. Under its auspices, the bishop's seat was located at St George's, Jerusalem, where the collegiate church (later cathedral), college, guest house and school were constructed and dedicated in 1898.

c   **The Development of Zionism and Christian Zionism**

6.24   Towards the end of the nineteenth century, many peoples in Europe were still ruled by the long-established empires of Austria-Hungary and Russia. The rise of democracy and industrialisation led to opposition to the old empires, a desire for national unity and autonomy based on language and culture. The unification of both Italy and of Germany and national independence movements such as those in the Balkans were the backdrop to the birth of political Zionism. Although the development of Zionism was the result of a number of factors, the rise of overt antisemitism, within a Europe which had appeared to welcome emancipation and encouraged assimilation, undoubtedly provided a major spur.

6.25   Tsarist Russia, which had continued to regard its Jewish population as unacceptable aliens, began a series of harsh measures and pogroms which led to mass migrations across Europe and to the United States. While religious Zionism – the fervent hope of an end to spiritual exile – had always existed, especially in poorer and pious religious communities, secularisers also began to consider longingly a future in *Zion*. Since Sir Moses Montefiore had rescued the Damascus Jewish community from persecution and re-established them just outside Jerusalem in 1840, such events were seen by some as models for possible repatriation.

6.26   The 1890s have often been seen as the period of growth of antipathy towards Jews and the increasing viewing of Jewish characteristics as being inimical to society or even nationhood.[55] The term *antisemitism* was coined by Wilhelm Marr in 1879. The pogroms and persecutions in Eastern Europe were matched by openly antisemitic societies in Germany and Austria, and the notorious case of Alfred Dreyfus in France. In this climate, Theodor Herzl, the Hungarian-born writer and journalist, wrote *Der Judenstaat*, proposing a national homeland for Jews, though not necessarily in Palestine. This approach caught the imagination of both wealthy and influential Jews and, to Herzl's surprise, the ordinary working class *Ostjuden* from Eastern Europe, who fêted him on his visit to London's East End. The First Zionist Congress took place in Basel in 1897 and included delegates from Britain.

6.27   It should be noted that there was considerable opposition, primarily from ultra-Orthodox quarters. For many religious Jews, human efforts to construct a Jewish society in Palestine represented a blasphemous usurpation by humans of a divine prerogative (this was described as being a violation of the *Three Oaths*[56] governing Israel's relation to the Gentiles according to God's purposes). The secular nature of Zionism and the zeal with which many ordinary Jews embraced it further increased this tension. On the other hand, most well-established Western Jews saw the movement as a retrograde step and their future as being members of European or American society.

6.28   Christian views differed, but many were of the opinion that Jews had a key role to play in eschatological hopes. One notable exponent of this was William Hechler, an Anglican priest who travelled widely as a missionary for CMS. In 1882, he travelled to Germany on behalf of the Church Pastoral Aid Society to investigate the situation of Jews. Hechler was particularly shocked by the results of the Russian pogroms. Having met with proponents of early Zionism, Hechler obtained a letter from Queen Victoria addressed to the Sultan of Turkey, calling upon him to permit the Jews to return to Palestine. However, the British Ambassador refused to present it. In 1884 Hechler wrote his own treatise, *The Restoration of the Jews to Palestine*, in which he argued that their restoration would pave the way for the Second Coming. The conversion of Jews to Christianity was not seen by Hechler as a necessary step. Pope St Pius X, on the other hand, told Herzl that, should Jews come to Palestine in large numbers, missionaries would be there waiting to convert them to Catholicism. He also stated that he could not sanction a Jewish state, because the Jews had refused to recognise Jesus.

6.29   Meanwhile in Palestine, Jewish immigration continued steadily. Significant groups of young idealistic, secular Jews from Europe began arriving. They were influenced by European socialist principles and keen to found utopian communities based on agriculture, physical labour and equality. Their approach, background and lifestyle contrasted dramatically with that of the dominant population – the agricultural-based Palestinian families, organised locally and with traditional family leaders. The new immigrants also had little in common with the small communities of religious Jews.

6.30   There was goodwill in Britain towards the Zionist cause. This arose both from concern at the influx of *Ashkenazi* (northern European, mostly Yiddish-speaking) refugees following the Russian pogroms and from a romantic view of Jewish aspirations, stirred up by the novels of Disraeli and George Eliot's popular *Daniel Deronda* (1876). Herzl came to meet Lord Rothschild, who was a member of the Royal Commission set up to advise on Jewish immigration. Initially sceptical, Rothschild was won over and proposed to the British government that while Jewish refugees should be given every assistance, the ultimate aim was to find them a permanent autonomous home abroad. From this point both the Colonial Secretary, Joseph Chamberlain, and the Foreign Secretary, Lord Lansdowne, began actively to look for a suitable territory. There were a number of proposals, including an area on the Egyptian border – to which Egypt objected – and Uganda. Lord Lansdowne wrote that, should a site agreeable to all be found, Her Majesty's Government would support the establishment of 'a Jewish colony of settlement, on conditions which will enable the members to observe their national customs'. [57]

6.31   The growth of Anglican congregations in Palestine led to the formation of the Palestinian Native Church Council in 1905. This was intended to give Palestinians more say in the running of the church and led to an increase in the number of Palestinian and Arab clergy serving the diocese. Although it mirrored a deliberate Ottoman policy to return more control to Arab hands, the Anglican Church was not officially recognised by the Ottoman administration, but was permitted under the Ottoman Law of Societies. Even when revisions were made in 1922 and 1939, Anglicans were not included. Under Bishop Macinnes, commitment to the ordination of Palestinian priests to serve in the region continued.

6.32   In 1914, Germany succeeded in gaining the support of the Turks in the tensions leading up to World War I. This resulted in Britain's determination to end Ottoman domination in the Middle East. Chaim Weizmann, a teacher of biochemistry at Manchester University from Eastern Europe and a fervent Zionist, was at this time introduced to members of the government including Lloyd George, Winston Churchill and Arthur Balfour. Together with the Liberal MP Samuel Herbert, who had experienced anti-semitism first-hand and seen the poverty of Jews in Whitechapel in London, Weizmann began a campaign for a national homeland within the area of the Middle East. Lloyd George was moved by the mention of biblical place names which figured in the discussions at this time, finding them to be 'more familiar than those on the Western Front'. [58] There was little support for Zionism generally in Britain at this time, even among the Jewish communal leadership, but supporters of Arab nationalism were less well organised. Lloyd George created a special Jewish Legion to fight as part of the British Army in the war in the Middle East region. In practice, they achieved little, but the Legion provided military training and experience. Meanwhile, the British and French governments, with the agreement of Russia, worked out a division of the Ottoman Empire giving Syria and Lebanon to France and dividing Palestine into areas of British and Anglo-French control. This was the Sykes-Picot agreement, which also committed the signatories to work for the independence of the Arab nations if the Arabs helped with the war effort.

6.33   In 1917, the British Cabinet agreed the wording of a statement known as the Balfour Declaration, in which they expressed their favour for the establishment of a Jewish homeland in Palestine. The Declaration did not give the campaigners all that they had hoped for; it mentioned neither administration nor immigration, but did state a commitment to safeguarding the rights of 'existing non-Jewish communities'. [59] British military experts in Palestine had strongly advised against such a Declaration. In London, Edwin Montagu, a prominent politician and leader in the Jewish community, warned that such a declaration would provide an excuse for countries to 'get rid of their Jews' by sending them to Palestine. He wrote to Lloyd George warning that Zionism played into antisemitic hands by implying that Jews were not contributors to British society but in effect belonged somewhere else. Nevertheless, at the peace negotiations following the First World War, Britain was given the Palestine mandate; the practicalities of controlling the region, with the growth of Arab nationalism and the overwhelming expectations of the Jewish population, were fraught with tremendous difficulties from the start. The early Mandate period saw increasing violence, and the deaths of hundreds of Jews and Arabs; in the riots in Hebron in 1929, over 60 Jews were killed.

6.34   In 1927 the Society of Jews and Christians was established in London to build positive relations between Christians and Jews. In 1930 the theologian James Parkes published *The Jew and His Neighbour*, which described the history of antisemitism, including the role played by Christianity in its terrible history. Parkes grew in influence and provided the intellectual background for initiatives in Jewish-Christian relations in Britain over the next decade. While working for the Student Christian Movement in Geneva, Parkes also witnessed the rise of Adolf Hitler and National Socialism. In 1942, as the Nazi regime began to implement their 'Final Solution' – the planned annihilation of Jews throughout Europe – the Archbishop of Canterbury, William Temple, met with the British Chief Rabbi, Joseph Hertz. Although as yet ignorant of the full thrust of Nazi activity towards Jews, they were concerned to encourage positive relations to prevent the worst excesses of antisemitism from taking hold in Britain; this led to the formation of the national Council of Christians and Jews.

6.35   By the end of the Second World War, around six million European Jews – men, women and children – had been deliberately and systematically murdered as part of Nazi strategy. This was a huge and outstanding act of human destruction.[60] Thousands more Jews were left traumatized, without families and homes. Many saw Palestine as a potential safe haven where they could live with other Jews, away from a Europe that plainly could not be trusted.[61] President Truman preferred that the refugees settle in Palestine rather than in the United States; there were, however, those who saw Jewish repatriation (that is, back within their European countries of origin) as the moral duty of Europe. The British government, which still had a mandate over Palestine, tried to limit Jewish immigration, following concern from local Arab leaders and other states in the region. However, intense pressure from immigrants and sympathetic international voices, together with the overwhelming desire for nationhood, resulted in armed Jewish resistance against British military rule. This came originally from Haganah, founded to defend local interest, but increasingly its more radical offshoots, the Irgun[62] and the Stern Gang, used terrorism and violence to deadly effect.

6.36   Post-Holocaust, Christians were forced to acknowledge that centuries of anti-Judaic rhetoric, including approaches such as supersessionism and the 'teaching of contempt' by the Church, had contributed to a mind-set which allowed the atrocities, in which millions of Jews were systematically targeted and murdered, to happen. The churches in Europe had been unprepared theologically to take a stand against the horrific acts. Even the early debates of the German Confessing Church had centred on issues of church autonomy rather than human rights. Many Christians, both clergy and laity, were recorded expressing the view that the sufferings of the Jews were the just recompense for their 'having killed Christ'. Such realisations led to widespread re-evaluation of Christian approaches to Jews and Judaism. Theologians such as Henry Cargas and Franklin Littell in the United States, personally devastated by attitudes perpetrated in the name of Christ, began to consider theologically what it meant to be Christian in the aftermath of the Holocaust.

d   Aftermath of Empire

6.37   From 1945, Britain found the cost and stress of administering the region overwhelming. Attempts to broker deals between Zionist and Arab leaders were inconclusive and the United Nations proposed a partition of Palestine into Jewish and Arab regions, the latter under the control of Jordan.[63] Jewish authorities were generally in favour of the idea of such a partition, despite the fact that Jerusalem remained outside the suggested Israeli border. Critics of the plan pointed out that the proposed division ceded more than half the land to a Jewish state, irrespective of the fact that much of this belonged to Muslim or Christian Arabs. Moreover, Arab inhabitants had not been granted the right to self-determination, unlike the inhabitants of the proposed Jewish state. There was therefore staunch opposition from Arab inhabitants of Palestine and from neighbouring countries, some of whom saw the proposal as a hurried way for the rest of the world to absolve itself from responsibility for a problem which it had created. Others were concerned about resources and administration, apart from the uncertainties about life in a divided land.

6.38   Prior to 1948 it is estimated that there were around 350,000 Palestinian Christians of different denominations living in the region. (A UN report puts the total population of the area at 1.9 million, with 32 percent Jews.[64]) At least four towns had a considerable Christian majority (Bethlehem, Beit Jala, Ramallah and Nazareth), while others such as Gaza, Ramleh, Lydda, Beisan, Shafa Amr and Akka had important Palestinian Christian concentrations. There were also significant percentages of Christians in mixed cities, such as Jerusalem, Haifa, Jaffa and Safed. Standards of living and education among the Christian population were generally high and the two major newspapers in Palestine prior to World War I were owned by Christians. Both had expressed concern as early as 1910 at the prospect of Jewish statehood in Palestine.

6.39   Protestant and Anglican missionaries, having worked with creditable success among the Arab populations of the Middle East for over a century, were also among those urging caution. There was, however, a significant number of Christians in Europe and the United States for whom 'restoration of the Jews to The Land' was seen as being ordained by Scripture; to have resisted it would in their view have been both sinful and futile. These restorationists saw the creation of the new state as both a fulfilment and a validation of the yet-unrealised Old Testament prophecies. Furthermore, they believed that to support the Jewish cause brought blessing, citing in support of this view a variety of biblical texts of which the best-known is probably Gen 12.3: 'He who blesses thee, I will bless; he who curses thee, I will curse.'

6.40   Between 1947 and 1948, the Haganah and other bodies implemented a series of systematic plans. While these were described as gaining and consolidating control of the region and strategic routes from 'the enemy', in practice they involved forced evictions of thousands of Arabs from villages and towns,[65] and the massacre of Palestinian Arabs at Deir Yassin stands out as an especially horrific event. Murderous attacks were also carried out on Jews by Arabs: the assault on the medical convoy travelling to the Hadassah hospital on Mount Scopus is recalled with particular bitterness. Failed international moves culminated in the British withdrawal, without any real resolution to the situation, in the early hours of 14 May 1948. The Jewish authorities immediately declared the establishment of the State of Israel; this is now commemorated as Independence Day by Israel. For Palestinians, it was a catastrophe, *Nakba*, and is commemorated as such.

6.41 Neighbouring Arab countries declared war on the new state. In the ensuing conflict, thousands more Palestinian Arabs fled from or were driven from their homes, in many cases thinking they would be back within days or weeks, locking their houses and taking the keys with them.[66] These were violent times. Many sought safety in neighbouring Arab countries, such as Syria, Lebanon and Jordan, as well as in Gaza and other local areas. They and their descendants have, in many cases, retained the status of refugees ever since. At the same time, hundreds of thousands of Jews were forced to leave Arab countries where they had lived for generations, identifying as 'Jewish Arabs', for haven in Israel. Empty Arab homes were used to house the growing number of Jewish immigrants to the region. Coming mostly from war-torn Europe, the new residents asked few questions at the time about the villages where they now lived. The Anglican Church, alongside others in the region, worked to cope with the war and the ensuing refugee problem as best it could, mostly through the use of church centres and by acting as a liaison and a 'missing persons' office wherever possible.

6.42 In 1947, the newly formed International Council of Christians and Jews issued a statement known as The Ten Points of Seelisburg. This was one of the first statements in which Christians, advised by and in consultation with Jews, openly addressed Christian approaches to Jews and Judaism following the Holocaust. Emphasising the Jewish roots of Christianity, the statement called upon Christians to reject anti-Judaic teaching such as blaming Jews for Christ's death and using pejorative descriptions both in relation to Jews of the New Testament and in the contemporary world. Other statements from various church bodies followed, but the most momentous was that in 1965 when, as a result of the Second Vatican Council, the Roman Catholic Church produced *Nostra Aetate*, followed up with *Notes and Guidelines*. Although concerned with approaches to all faiths, its tremendous influence was felt mostly in the field of relations with Jews. It both marked a milestone in changes of attitudes and provided the imperative for a reappraisal of Catholic teaching. *Nostra Aetate* emphasised both the cross of Christ as showing the centrality of God's love for all humanity and the need for mutual respect across faiths, while rejecting language and approaches which denigrated Judaism. It is worth noting that the question of *the Land* or the State of Israel did not feature in Christian-Jewish dialogue or church documents until after *Nostra Aetate*.

6.43 The Theology Committee of the International Council of Christians and Jews also laid the groundwork for a number of initiatives. Perhaps the most notable of these was *Dabru Emet* ('Speak Truth') 2001, a statement by a number of Jewish scholars and rabbis, predominantly from the United States, acknowledging Christian attempts at dialogue. Among paragraphs about the Bible, Torah principles and the Holocaust, the document includes one on Israel, stating that Christian support for Israel should be 'applauded', and recognising the Jewish tradition of having regard for all those, both Jews and non-Jews, who live there.

e **Zionists and Palestinians**

6.44 In the ensuing decades, a number of wars and violent conflicts between Israel and its Arab neighbours, and incursions into Israel, took place. There were, of course, political and social aspects to these on which Christians were divided. From a theological perspective, many Christians internationally, whether engaged in dialogue with Jews or not, tended to regard these events as purely political and beyond the scope of general Church life and worship. Some saw the need to support Israel as a biblical command, and a significant number of groups were formed which met specifically to pray for Israel's military and economic success. Other Christian voices were raised in concern about war and violence as a whole; some called for moral accountability, and stressed the tradition of the prophets in commending social justice. The Council of Christians and Jews in Britain minuted its concern at the failure of Arab states to make peace with Israel. It also noted some alarm at the Israeli attack on Qibya, near the Jordan border, in 1953.

6.45   By 1964, a resurgent sense of Palestinian national identity among the Arab inhabitants of Gaza and the West Bank (as well as the many Arabs holding Israeli citizenship), was given political voice through the establishment of the Palestine Liberation Organisation (PLO). Tensions between Israel and its neighbours rose. In 1967 these tensions culminated in the build-up of military forces on Israel's borders, together with a blockade of Eilat, setting off what has become known as The Six Day War. Israel launched a pre-emptive strike, recognising that defeat would almost certainly have brought an effective end to the state and its infrastructure. As a result of the war, Israel took possession of the Old City of Jerusalem, East Jerusalem, the West Bank, Gaza and the Sinai Peninsula. The free access of Jews to their holiest site – the Western Wall of the Temple Mount – was a sign for rejoicing for Jews throughout the world, shared by many Christians, including, though not exclusively, those who saw this as being of eschatological significance. The war of 1967 is seen as a watershed moment in terms of how debate on Israel developed both internationally and for Christians, including effects on diaspora Jews. The United Nations Security Council passed Resolution 242[67] calling for withdrawal 'from territories occupied in the recent conflict' and emphasised 'the inadmissibility of the acquisition of territory by war', a view echoed by the World Council of Churches. The Resolution also called for an end to belligerency and a commitment to respecting the sovereignty of states, with their right to live peacefully within secure borders. This Resolution has formed the basis of most subsequent peace negotiations.

6.46   Over the next few years, under the leadership of Yasser Arafat, the Palestine Liberation Organization carried out a number of high-profile terrorist activities, including international hijackings and murder of Jews, before totally renouncing terrorism in 1988. The war in 1973, known as the Yom Kippur War, was another in which defeat for Israel by its neighbours would have effectively meant the end of the State. While Sinai was progressively returned to Egypt following the Camp David agreement of 1978,[68] the West Bank has remained under Israeli military occupation. During the course of these events, many Christians have been vocal in their support for *either* Palestinians *or* Israeli Jews while also denouncing the other, thus encouraging a growing polarisation within the churches. This polarisation increased due to Israel's wars in Lebanon, first in 1982 and later in 2006. Even though such wars may have been a response to provocation by Palestinian or Arab groups, it was not feasible for Israel to portray its invasions into Lebanon, and the concomitant considerable loss of civilian life, as primarily defensive actions.

6.47   In 1957 the Anglican presence in Jerusalem was restructured as an archbishopric, under the extra-Provincial jurisdiction of the Archbishop of Canterbury. It was led by an expatriate archbishop who oversaw the whole of the Middle East. The first Arab bishop, Najib Cubain, was consecrated as Bishop of Jordan, Lebanon and Syria, including the West Bank. Though based in Jerusalem, he did not have any formal episcopal authority in the city itself. Between 1974 and 1976, the archbishopric was completely restructured again and the Diocese of Jerusalem was established in January 1976 to include Palestine, Jordan, Israel, Lebanon and Syria, with Jerusalem as its centre, and with its bishop co-titled as the Anglican Bishop in Jerusalem and Bishop of the Episcopal Diocese of Jerusalem. Two Palestinian assistant bishops had been consecrated in 1974, one based in Amman and the other, as coadjutor, based in Jerusalem. The latter, Faiq Haddad, was enthroned as Bishop of the Diocese of Jerusalem in 1976.

6.48 Following the 1967 war, large numbers of Jews and those of Jewish descent from Eastern Europe took advantage of the Israeli Law of Return under which anyone with a Jewish grandparent (which had also been the Nazi categorisation of those sent to the camps) could apply for citizenship. (This law has been a further cause of animosity for Palestinian refugees who are unable to return to villages they had lived in for generations.) The fall of the Soviet Union in 1990 resulted in increased numbers of immigrants to Israel. Between 1987 and 1993 the *First Intifada* or Palestinian uprising took place. Palestinians organised opposition to Israel mostly through boycotts, strikes and barricades, as well as by organised groups of stone-throwing youths.

6.49 Serious theological attempts to consider the situation were illuminated by Liberation Theology. Originating in Latin America, this emphasised the centrality of social and political liberation in the work and purpose of the Kingdom of God. The Sabeel Ecumenical Liberation Theology Centre in Jerusalem, founded and directed by an Anglican priest, Canon Naim Ateek,[69] has continued to develop this within the Palestinian context.[70] An undergirding principle of the vision of Sabeel is that justice and peace cannot be separated. Sabeel holds regular conferences for international groups in Jerusalem and the West Bank: in 2004 such a conference focused specifically on the topic of Christian Zionism.

6.50 The increase in number of ideological Jewish immigrants, supported by Israeli government policy, has encouraged the continued building and expansion of controversial 'settlements'– townships within the occupied West Bank which are exclusively for Jewish citizens of Israel and to which considerable government resources are diverted. The expansion of such settlements is illegal under international law.[71] Not all residents of settlements are ideologically driven by any means; for many, these neighbourhoods are simply available and convenient. However, others believe fervently that it is their religious duty to live in and control the land which God promised to Abraham's Hebrew descendants. Alongside this is the belief of many Christians – especially but not exclusively conservative evangelical groups – that support for Israel and Jewish migration is also their religious duty. This belief has arisen either from eschatological views or from a strict adherence to texts such as Genesis 12.3. The growth in influence of such groups, predominantly in the United States, is credited by many with driving Western political policies in the region.

6.51 A number of church documents and reports, including from the World Council of Churches, have addressed the situation. In 2002 an initiative of the then Archbishop of Canterbury, George Carey, led to the Alexandria Declaration, signed by Jewish, Christian and Muslim leaders in the region, which called on 'the political leaders of both peoples to work for a just, secure and durable solution in the spirit of the words of the Almighty and the Prophets'.[72] There have also been serious international attempts to broker peace – primarily the Camp David Accords in 2000, treaties with Egypt and Jordan in 1979 and 1994 respectively, and the Oslo Accords (1993). Although causes for hope, the reasons for the failures of these measures to achieve a breakthrough depend on complex factors, many of which are disputed on all sides.

6.52   In terms of inter faith relations and the Anglican Communion, the Lambeth Conference of 1988 accepted the document *Jews, Christian and Muslims: The Way of Dialogue* (which appeared in the final report *The Truth Shall Make You Free* as an appendix).[73] The document condemned 'aggressive' attempts at proselytisation, which was a major concern for Jews at the time. It also called for genuine dialogue and a willingness to share and to learn from the other, as well as emphasising the concern both Jews and Christians shared – to honour God's name. The Anglican Communion's Network for Inter Faith Concerns (NIFCON) was also charged with promoting positive Christian-Muslim relations. In 2001, the Inter Faith Consultative Group of the Archbishops' Council produced 'a contribution to a continuing debate': '*Sharing One Hope?*' *The Church of England and Christian-Jewish Relations*. In addition to an overview of the history of such relations, and an examination of current concerns, the booklet included a short section on the State of Israel. Following its examination of the issues confronting Christians in this situation, the chapter concluded that while Anglicans can and do hold strong opinions on the issues, 'their views should be tempered by the recognition that they do not have to live directly with the consequences, as do Arabs and Jews in the Middle East'.[74] In 2007, the Archbishop of Canterbury, Dr Rowan Williams, together with the Chief Rabbis of Israel, inaugurated the Anglican-Jewish Commission to promote theological dialogue and increased understanding. The Commission has continued to meet regularly.[75] A similar commission for dialogue, established in 2001 between the Anglican Communion and the *Al-Azhar Al-Sharif*, the significant centre of Muslim learning and jurisprudence based in Cairo, has also met regularly during the past decade. The need for peace and reconciliation in Israel/Palestine and the importance of religious leaders acting as peace makers in situations of conflict such as exists in the Holy Land, has been a regular item of discussion among Anglicans and Muslims during their meetings.[76]

Chapter 7

Some key theological issues – gift, return, city

7.1 We believe that any Christian understanding of the Holy Land must attend with the utmost seriousness to the presence of the Christian community in that land. As we shall see, this presence cannot be without that of other communities, Jews and Muslims in particular. In fact, it is because we take seriously the physical reality of Christians in Israel/Palestine that we also have to honour the physical reality of others' claims on the land. Nevertheless, for us the starting point must be the importance of sustaining Christian life in the land of Jesus, as the Archbishop of Canterbury has pointed out:

> Christianity is an historical religion: at the centre of Christian faith is a set of events which occurred in a particular place at a particular time… Christians are answerable, they are responsible, to what happened in the Holy Land two millennia ago; they go back to be questioned and enlarged, to be challenged and inspired, by specific events, and the connection of Christians now with those specific events two thousand years ago is a vital part of Christian faith. In that perspective, the continuity of Christian worship and witness in the places where these events occurred is not a small thing for Christian believers. It is a kind of gnosticism… a kind of cutting loose from history if we say that the presence of our brothers and sisters in the land of Our Lord does not matter to us.[77]

7.2 Archbishop Rowan's reference here to 'a kind of gnosticism' is significant, because one characteristic of gnosticism is that it involves a divorce of the material from the spiritual. For Christian faith, by contrast, the Incarnation asserts the union of the material and the spiritual in Christ. The Archbishop's words also underline the relationship between the particular and the universal: in contrast to a gnostic tendency to abstraction, Christian faith affirms that the particular circumstances of the Incarnation continue to be of importance precisely because they are of universal significance. In trying to set out a Christian understanding of the Holy Land, then, we need to hold together both the material and the spiritual, and also the particular and the universal. Not only are these joined in the Incarnation, but we shall also see that an Anglican understanding of the sacramental principle continues to link both.

7.3 In thinking further about what it means in concrete terms to value and to sustain Christian presence in the Holy Land, we can identify three key biblical motifs which are unavoidable in shaping a theologically informed understanding, and which have been intensively discussed by Christian Zionists, as well as by Christians with anti-Zionist views. These three are:

- first, the relationship between the Land known as Israel and the people called Israel, a relationship which has been described as that between a gift and its recipients;
- second, the successive themes of exile and return;
- third, the Holy City of Jerusalem, and within that the Temple.

How can each of these be interpreted, in light of a characteristic Anglican approach which holds together the material and the spiritual, and the particular and the universal, while recognising the centrality of Christian presence?

a   The Gift of the Land

7.4   There are two simple ways, neither of them satisfactory for an Anglican methodology, of interpreting the biblical theme of the gift of the Land of Israel. On the one hand, Christian Zionism takes very seriously the materiality and particularity of that gift, seeing it as a once for all, unconditional and irrevocable, grant to the Jewish people through Abraham. One dramatically pictorial account, for example, talks of God driving the 'original stakes' into the soil of Judea.[78] Many centuries later, and after countless vicissitudes, it is argued, the reality of this grant has been confirmed in human history by the establishment of the State of Israel, which has definitively established Jewish sovereignty over the Land in accordance with God's original and unchanging purpose. Politically, the Land of Israel does and should belong to the Jewish people, and this political actuality is the confirmation of the divine truth to which the Bible, rightly interpreted, bears witness. In the most tightly defined versions of Christian Zionism, this argument from biblical interpretation relies on a dispensationalist reading of the Bible, at the core of which is a sharp division made between, on the one hand, the original material promise made to the people of Israel, which continues in force throughout the Christian dispensation, and on the other hand a separate, spiritual covenant made through Christ with the Church.

7.5   On the other hand, through much of Christian history, although traditional views held through much of Christian history have agreed with the starting point of this approach, in its emphasis on the materiality of the original grant of the Land to Abraham and his descendants. However, they have drawn from this very different conclusions. The continuing validity of the grant is then seen as being subsequently cancelled by Israel's disobedience to God's message, culminating in the rejection of the Messiah by the Jewish people; it is therefore an expression of God's purposes, according to this view, that that people should be displaced from the land which had been promised to them. The 'Land' then becomes generalised into the whole world, as the first people Israel are entirely replaced in God's purposes by the Christian Church, which spreads throughout the whole earth; the particular is succeeded by the universal, and at the same time the promise of the land is evacuated of its physical content. We can see here an abrogation of the material in favour of the spiritual, and a replacement of the particular by the universal, resulting in a theology whose content is indeed directly contradictory to the Christian Zionist reading; nevertheless, the two readings have much in common in their methodologies, which both in different ways dissociate the material from the spiritual.

7.6   An approach which begins from the material actuality of Christian presence in the Holy Land will differ in major ways from both these viewpoints, that of *Christian Zionism* and that which we might call *displacement theology*. It is our conviction that the nature of our Christian faith, with its commitment to the *scandal of particularity* in the incarnation, requires us to hold in creative tension both the material and spiritual, the particular and the universal, and suggests that incarnation does not invalidate the significance of chosenness but can be a pathway which allows it to open out to incorporate a wider and more inclusive vision. For Christians, maintaining presence in the Holy Land has a vital significance in three related ways, none of which can be simply described in terms of a theological theory; on the contrary, they represent the lived reality of Christian faith.

7.7   First, there is a holiness in the soil and stones marked by Jesus' earthly life, the place of his death, the site from which his resurrection is first proclaimed; the Incarnation, as it transforms the material through the spiritual, has made particular places holy through their being touched by the physical presence of the Lord. This sense of a sanctity of place for Christians also reaches back for Christians before Jesus' earthly life into the story of the people to whom he belonged: the scenes of God's interaction with the people of biblical Israel are also recognised as holy sites by Christians.

7.8 Second, in response to that holiness, from early centuries onwards the holy places, both those associated with the life of Jesus and those linked to the Old Testament theophanies, became the goal of Christian pilgrimage. Throughout the centuries, the people of Jesus have travelled from across the world to touch the places that he touched, to know at first hand the geography that he inhabited, to enter through their own experience into the history that was his. The Land itself has sometimes been described as the 'Fifth Gospel', and like the four written Gospels it continues to engage the imagination of Christian pilgrims of every background, who have returned carrying with them the associations of holiness to re-imagine their own home landscapes as holy lands. Yet pilgrimage is no purely spiritual exercise divorced from political realities: access to the holy sites has been an issue of dispute and contest throughout the Christian centuries, and remains so now.

7.9 Third, and most immediately for us now, the Christian communities of the Holy Land continue to live out the life of the Body of Christ in the very places where Jesus lived. It is imperative for sustaining Christian presence in Israel/Palestine that this is not merely a curatorial role, but shows the living reality of the universal Church in this unique locality; as the remarks quoted above (7.1) point out, if we do not value and sustain Christian presence in the Holy Land, we fall into a kind of gnosticism. The political issues involved here are even more contentious than those which arise from access to the pilgrimage sites, and the challenge to the worldwide church is all the more pressing.

7.10 Christian presence in the Holy Land, then, is central to our own story, and it has its own distinctive characteristics. These are different from those distinctive themes which mark the Jewish presence in Israel, and different also from the patterns of presence of other religious communities in Israel/Palestine – notably, Muslim communities, but also Baha'i, Druze and others. However we believe that what we have said about the importance of Christian presence can offer a paradigm for Christian reflection on Jewish under-standing of the 'gift of the land', acknowledging that here too the *scandal of particularity* needs to be taken seriously by Christians. Yet as with our understanding of Christian presence itself it is vital that particularity and chosenness in Jewish understanding of the 'gift of the land' opens the door to a vision that goes beyond itself. The attachment and longing of Jews for *eretz Israel* over the centuries may be unparalleled in its intensity and depth, and the contemporary imperative for the security of their presence cannot be questioned; but the Jewish presence can only be affirmed by churches around the world in ways that also give space for others to be present, their fellow Christians included. In thinking further about what that might mean for our interpretation of the gift of the Land as that is set out in the biblical narrative, three points can be mentioned: what it means to give such a gift; the basis on which the gift is given; and the nature of land as gift. For each, there are resources from Anglicanism which can help us with our thinking.

7.11 The giving of the land should not be isolated as a one-off isolated event, divorced from the rest of human history. Rather, it is a story of the continuing bringing into relationship with God of a people and community who sanctify the Land by their presence, so that it becomes a place where God's voice is heard, prophetic messages are received, the identity of a people is worked out, and a network of places is marked by narrative and biographical associations. In their relations with Jewish people, it is the density and attachment of Israel's interactions with the Land that we believe Christians should acknowledge and affirm; rather than focusing on a sheer act of grant to Abraham, we trace the many ways in which his descendants have been at home in the lands of which Genesis speaks. Within the Old Testament taken as a whole, no single theology of the Land, no single account of its gift, can be identified.

7.12 A significant study of models of land in the Old Testament, *The Land is Mine*, by the Australian Christian scholar Norman Habel, posits six different models of *land ideology* offered in different parts of the Old Testament: land as the source of wealth: a royal ideology; land as conditional grant: a theocratic ideology; land as family lots: an ancestral household ideology; land as God's personal heritage (*nahalah*): a prophetic ideology; land as Sabbath bound: an agrarian ideology; land as host country: an immigrant ideology. These differing models can and do stand in tension and conflict with each other within scripture, a reality that suggests that an oversimplistic or uncritical dependence by Christians on particular Old Testament biblical verses when seeking biblical warrant for modern political dispensations in Israel/Palestine is perhaps less than fully biblical. Given the particular use of the Abraham narratives in at least some forms of Christian Zionism (see eg 4.1), it is interesting to note specifically that it is this ideology which, in Habel's analysis, shows most sympathy for the indigenous inhabitants of the land to which Abraham came as an immigrant. In the Abraham narratives these indigenous inhabitants are seen as 'hosts', and in none of Abraham's dealings with these peoples is their right to possess the land put in question. 'Abraham is a peaceful immigrant who willingly recognizes the land entitlements of the peoples of the host country. Even the promises to Abraham about future possession of the land focus on Abraham mediating blessing to other families of the land, rather than on the annihilation of his hosts.'[79]

7.13 Other communities also have a history of interaction with, attachment to and aspiration for the Land of Israel. Some Palestinians today re-read elements of the Old Testament narratives in self-identification with ancient Canaanite inhabitants, and Palestinian readings of the history of this land can also be generated through reliance on archaeological evidence, which may at times point in a direction contrary to the biblical narrative. It is clear that the story of this land has through the centuries been contested by different groups seeking to maintain their own presence. When that presence is seen as being given for the purpose of building a relationship with and a witness to God, it becomes apparent that space needs to be given to other groups also, so that in their presence too the reality of God's presence may be acknowledged.

7.14 This leads us on to the basis on which the gift is made: for the Land is not at all given without any responsibilities attached to it. Although the gift is purely gratuitous, it carries with it the imperative to those who receive it of engagement with others in the cause of spreading God's message of justice, truth and righteousness. This is the message of the prophets, who positively link the gift of the Land to a divine mission to the nations; negatively, this becomes the theme of conditionality, so that disobedience attenuates or even cancels the relationship established by the gift – in vivid imagery, the Torah even refers to the land 'vomiting out' the people if they are disobedient (Lev 18.28). It is also notable that most biblical promises of land are precisely that – promises, with a necessary future orientation, calling into question whether one can or should speak of *fulfilment* of the gift in the present. A nuanced understanding of biblical eschatology calls into question both restorationist and dispensationalist models of Christian Zionism.

7.15 A number of early Zionists (eg Abraham Isaac Kook; Martin Buber)[80] held a view of restoration to the Land as a mission to restore the people, and to create a society from which light and truth could spread to the world. In the early years of the Israeli state, this high expectation was also present. It may seem unrealistic to expect any political reality to conform to the exalted standards of divine law to a higher degree than other nations; yet it is entirely right to expect all the jurisdictions of the Holy Land to abide by basic principles of human rights, which have their roots in the teachings that have spread from this land.

7.16 As to the nature of that which is given – no land in human history is to be thought of as a bare physical object; rather, it always comes with populations attached to it. Lands are given as places for human flourishing, which means that hospitality must be practised by each to all other inhabitants of the Land, whether in one's own community or 'the other'. This is embedded in the Old Testament in the injunctions to treat with respect and welcome the *gerim*,[81] those described as 'resident aliens' who as guests share the land with the Jewish people who traced their descent as Israel from the patriarchs. Indeed, they were continually reminded that the condition of guesthood was central to their own formative story: it was as a *ger* that Abraham had himself received the promise of the Land from God. In this vision, flourishing is mandated in the land for all people, and also for animals and for the environment itself: practising God's hospitality involves ecological stewardship.

7.17 The presuppositions of hospitality are themselves loaded: the questions, who has the right to be counted as host, who is cast in the role of guest, carry clear political implications. At different times in the last two millennia, Jewish, pagan, Christian and Muslim powers have been in positions of dominance; yet it is clear that there has never been a Holy Land without people who could justly claim an attachment to the land, never a so-called *terra nullius*. The slogan of 'a land without a people for a people without a land' was a travesty of the truth if taken to mean that Palestine was unpopulated. A more nuanced version used it to deny nationhood to the Palestinians: the Jews, it was argued, were a coherent nation without territory, whereas the Palestinians were just a disparate group of people who happened to live in the area of Palestine. This is an untenable attitude; the reality of Palestinian peoplehood needs recognising along with the strength of their attachment to the land. Since 1967, the necessity of this recognition means in particular bringing an end to the Israeli occupation of Palestinian territory acquired in the Six Day War. This is an imperative made increasingly urgent by the continuing establishment of settlements and the construction of a divisive separation barrier, whose contours means that it has *de facto* become a means of annexing Palestinian territory. International justice, and the resolution of conflicts between peoples, depend on the consensus of nations, and imperfect though it may be the United Nations, with its Security Council, constitutes the best expression of this consensus in our world: its resolutions in relation to Israel/Palestine need to be honoured.

7.18 However, the relationship of peoples to land should not be conceived of in a static or purely territorial way; populations are flows of people as well as settled communities, and the challenge facing Israel/Palestine today is to welcome and accommodate not only indigenous Jews and Arabs, but also newly arrived communities from across the world, Jewish and *Gentile*. This movement of peoples is of course itself not uncontroversial. On the one hand the Law of Return facilitates Jewish immigration freely; on the other hand the right of return for Palestinian refugees is not accepted. Yet among those coming to the land are many Christians, and, particularly in Israel, relating to the new presence of these migrant communities of fellow believers is a challenging experience for the historic churches of the Holy Land. Always, though, the gift of the Land is a gift to enable mutual hospitality, to create a place of universal welcome where the people of all nations can be welcomed: those whose ancestry lies in this particular land, those who are new migrants, those who travel on pilgrimage and those who are returning from exile.

b   **Exile and return**

7.19   The themes of an exile from the land of promise, and of a longing to return there, fore-shadowed even in the Pentateuch, are dominant in the later part of the biblical narrative of Israel, and have echoed throughout Jewish history also. At one level, this is a matter of geographical dispersion and ingathering; yet physical exile and return are motifs which carry strong spiritual resonances also, and they are not limited to the experience of Jewish people. The state of exile, *galut*, while it may be seen as a consequence of disobedience to God's laws on the part of the community living in the promised land, comes also to have a positive significance in Jewish life and spirituality. For example, Jeremiah urges the exiles to seek the welfare of the city in which they live, and later rabbinic spirituality develops the idea of the divine glory, the *shekhinah*, travelling into exile with God's people. At no point, either in the Holy Land or in exile, does God abandon his people; while the promise of return is held out as an evident sign of God's favour in the future, in the meantime Israel continues always to be within his providential care. It is perhaps indicative of this ambiguous value of living in the land that, whereas the Hebrew Scriptures in their traditional arrangement (the *Tanakh*) end with Cyrus' proclamation of the return to Jerusalem, the Pentateuch closes with the death of Moses in Moab, outside Israel.[82]

7.20   The sense of a community in exile echoes strongly through the story of the Christian church. Early Christians, fervently longing for a homeland promised them in the kingdom of heaven, knew that they were strangers and pilgrims in the earthly cities where they were scattered. It is deeply embedded within scripture and tradition that the primary identity for Christians is to be discovered in the community of faith, rather than in ethnic belonging or geographical location. A sense of earthly life as exile has continued strong in the measure that eschatological expectation has remained lively: 'Now in the meantime, with hearts raised on high, we for that country must yearn and must sigh, seeking Jerusalem, dear native land, through our long exile on Babylon's strand'.[83] As with Judaism, this has not necessarily led Christians to a devaluing of the earthly city, but rather to a critical distance from unquestioning acceptance of its norms. In a post-Christendom era, the sense of Christians being in internal exile in their own societies has perhaps become even stronger. Yet there are also many for whom displacement from home is not a mere metaphor but a lived reality. Christian asylum seekers, refugees and migrants around the world find the biblical texts on exile speak powerfully to them today. Most importantly for us as Anglicans, many of our Palestinian brothers and sisters in the faith know in their own lives the pain of separation from the place they call home; we cannot close our ears to the longing of displaced Palestinians, Christians and Muslims to return from exile to their homeland. Palestinian poets, both Muslim and Christian, speak of their pain in passionate language which resonates powerfully with this motif of exile and return:

> Whether my way leads to a jail under the sun, or in exile.
> I shall not despair.
> It is my right to behold the sun, to demolish the tent and the banishment,
> To eat the fruit of the olive, to water the vineyards with music,
> To sing of love, in Jaffa, in Haifa, to sow the fertile land with new seeds.
> It is my right.[84]

7.21   Within these complex, multi-faceted and deeply felt Jewish and Christian experiences of exile, what account can we give of the project of return which resulted in the formation of the State of Israel? The early Zionists who pioneered this movement in the diaspora communities saw settlement in Palestine not only as a geographical move with demographic implications, nor even simply a place of safety from persecution, but also as a moral transformation. It was to generate a new way of being Jewish, in which innovative communities would shape their own destinies instead of being dependent on the good or ill will of others as in the *galut* experience. This in turn meant that they were to rely on their own, human, resources to achieve self-sufficiency, rather than waiting on the will of God to effect their restoration to the land. Thus the Zionist movement posed sharply to Jews the question of agency in relation to the return. Early Zionism was a secular, at times anti-religious, project, seeing the Jewish people themselves as agents of their own return; the colonial and mandatory powers were to be enlisted as secondary agents to help with this human project (or to be opposed if they tried to stop it). Many traditional Jews strongly objected to this approach, seeing it as a blasphemous usurpation of divine agency, as well as a denial of the divine significance of the *galut*, which had paradoxically become for them a sign of divine favour – the loving chastisement of the people of Israel by the God to whom they belonged.

7.22   There still remain Jews who are anti-Zionist on religious grounds, and there continues to be disagreement as to whether or not the State of Israel implies the advent of the Messianic times. However, since the foundation of the State in 1948, and particularly since the 1967 war, the rise of religious Zionism has seen various ways of reconciling the tension between secular Zionism and traditional Judaism. There is now a widespread sense among religious Jews that the return of God's people to their ancient homeland must be seen as a demonstration of his continuing action on their behalf in human history, however that may be understood in detail.

7.23   In this respect, religious (Jewish) Zionism converges with Christian Zionism, where the question of divine agency is not seriously contested. For Christian Zionists, the return of the Jews and the establishment of the State of Israel are seen as fulfilment of prophecy. They are also seen as signs of the beginning of the end times: restoration, the creation of a renewed community of worshippers as a prelude to the return of the Messiah. Christian Zionists differ considerably among themselves over the point at which any conversion of the Jews to Christianity fits into this process of restoration, but they tend to share in a detailed exegesis of the scriptures taken as a precise predictor of events.

7.24   As opposed to both religious Jewish and Christian Zionist interpretations of the return from exile and the formation of the State of Israel, many other Christians hold that these events are of purely secular moment. Such a view may rest on a general position that holds back from any attempt to identify a theological significance to any historical events, believing that this runs the risk of implicating God too closely in the contested realm of human *realpolitik*. For others, the refusal to ascribe any religious value to the establishment of modern Israel rests on a specific judgement that the Jewish people have no continuing place in God's plan, as this has now been taken by the Christian Church. Many also point out that the dispossession of Palestinian families and communities which attended these events was in fact a *nakba*, a catastrophe or disaster; it is, they say, impossible to discern the purposes of God in events like this, and it is dangerous to attempt to do so.

7.25   In view of these sharply contrasting readings, is it possible to find an interpretation of history and of scripture which recognises the patterns which are significant for Zionism, which gives them some theological value and critique, which avoids an unconvincingly detailed level of interpretation and which also recognises the sufferings of Palestinian and other communities adversely affected by the Zionist project? Anglican theology has stressed the discernment of a divine purpose in history, enabling those with faith to discern signs of God's activity in post-biblical times, in ways which are congruent with the indications given by scripture, but without attempting to read off a detailed historical programme from the canon of revelation. Discernment of this kind has been formatively shaped by the African bishop St Augustine, author of the *City of God*. Augustine appealed to what he called divine providence as a hermeneutic key to the events of his time. He wrote with a double motive: to defend the church against the criticism of pagans that the collapse of Roman power followed the abandonment of the old gods, but also to criticise those Christian historians who saw the conversion of the Empire as visible proof of the triumph of Christianity. Against their view that the purposes of God could be decoded from contemporary history by correlating them with scripture, Augustine insisted that, outside the biblical period, historical interpretation was necessarily a matter of discernment, built on an overall sense of the good purposes of God for humanity. He saw in history two realities, an earthly city and a heavenly, theologically separable but in actuality intertwined, and distinguished not as different dispensations but by their different motivations. Providence works in the interaction of the two, as the City of God moves ambiguously towards its heavenly goal.

7.26   Following Augustine's method, when we leave the biblical period to seek discernment of theological patterns in recent events, we will take seriously the evident resonances between the working out of the Zionist project and the pages of scripture, without looking for a precise correspondence. We will also take to heart those biblical episodes which speak of disaster and dispossession for God's people, of *nakba*; belief in God's providential oversight does not exclude the reality of disaster and lament. Such a reading, knowing God to be concerned with the whole of human history, will hold together in tension the biblical and the secular, without driving a wedge between them. Recognising that all peoples and communities are embraced within God's loving care, covered by the mandate of his justice, it will rule out any exclusive readings of history. Rather, it will insist that any theological reading of human history based on a biblical foundation must be informed by ethical imperatives which flow from recognition of the divine goodness, generosity and justice which the scriptures attest.

7.27   Such a historically enmeshed theology will rely on the Anglican principle of interpreting scripture in the light of tradition and reason. The post-Reformation Anglican emphasis on *sola scriptura* involves a restriction of primary theological sources to the text of the Bible in a way which refuses to elevate other principles, whether ecclesiastical tradition, confessional documents, or private inspiration, into authorities on the same level. By contrast, much Christian Zionist interpretation is an unwarranted eisegesis which does not do justice to the notes of agnosticism about the end times in the Bible. The modesty of the *sola scriptura* principle is further shown in the insistence that the only history which can be read unambiguously as the record of God's direct dealings is that limited to the biblical canon. Cognitive humility as an Anglican characteristic is rooted in scripture.

7.28   In interpreting the scriptures, Anglicans appeal to the consensus of tradition, which speaks of a *sensus plenior*, a meaning conveyed by the Bible as a whole, centrally focused on the person and work of Jesus Christ. This is in contrast to a dispensationalist methodology, which relies in large measure on the atomistic analysis of individual texts, distinguishing between those that apply to the earthly Israel and those that apply to the spiritual Church. While this ostensibly honours the integrity of the Old Testament, it actually drives a wedge between the two covenants. On the other hand, an approach which regards the material teachings of the Old Testament as superseded by the spiritual truths of the New is in danger of falling into the same trap. Against such divisions, Anglican tradition insists on the unity of the two scriptures:

> The Old Testament is not contrary to the New; for both in the Old and New Testament everlasting life is offered to Mankind by Christ... Wherefore they are not to be heard, which feign that the old Fathers did look only for transitory promises.[85]

7.29 The principle that reason plays a key part in the interpretation of scripture affirms the place of natural justice in exegesis. The inseparability of ethics from interpretation, which underpins the doctrine of providence, emphasises that God's concern is for all peoples, and so excludes any reading of scripture which is deliberately one-sided, focusing only on the benefit of the earthly Israel. An ethical concern for integrity will also resist any instrumentalisation of Jewish people so that they only have the significance given them by Christian theorising. An ethically informed exegesis will also eschew the relentless pessimism which insists that a violent outcome is God's final line in the apocalyptic drama. While being open to eschatology, it will refuse to accept that a conflictual outcome is either desirable or inevitable. Christian communities in the Holy Land, Anglicans among them, know that their biblically mandated vocation is to make peace, to work for justice and to seek reconciliation.

c   Holy City and Temple

7.30 For Christians, Jerusalem is the point at which the decisive action of God in Jesus Christ reached its climax; it was there that the Lord suffered, died, and was raised to new life, and that alone gives the city a focal sanctity for Christians around the world. For Jesus as a Jew, Jerusalem was already holy, the 'city of the great King', yet he was also well aware that this same city could be violent and sinful, the place where God's prophets were killed and where he would himself be killed. The community of Christians in Jerusalem was held in reverence in the apostolic Church, and in later centuries the city became a goal for Christian pilgrims from across the world, as it remains today. Even for those who have not made the physical journey, the holy city is, in virtually every tradition of Christianity, a symbol of hope and holiness; but it has also been the scene of warfare and massacre in the name of Christ, and of dissension between rival Christian groups. For the many different Christian communities resident in the city, Jerusalem today provides the ordinary context of their everyday lives, bringing all the stresses and challenges of a tense and divided city.

7.31 Before the Christ event and after it too, Jerusalem has always occupied a hugely important place in Judaism. For Jews around the world it has been and it is a focus of longing and aspiration, as well as being a place in which many have chosen to live, and to die and be buried. In the Old Testament, the city is hymned as a place of supreme beauty, of unquestioned centrality to the world, of invincible security. All of these themes flow theologically from the central affirmation that Jerusalem is uniquely selected by the eternal God, the place which he has chosen for his name to dwell. This idea, which may have been adopted from Canaanite theology, is affirmed particularly in the Psalms, and it is linked to the ideology of Davidic kingship. This royal 'presence theology' is held in tension with the message delivered by some of the prophets, who spoke of judgement and destruction for the city, and of exile for its citizens, though they also held out the promise of restoration and reconstruction.

7.32   At the heart of Jerusalem stood the Temple, where the reality of God's presence was almost tangible. In each period of exile, the Temple was destroyed, and following the trauma of 70 AD it was not rebuilt. From that time onwards, rabbinic Judaism became established as the normative religious expression of Jewish life worldwide, centred on the local synagogue and accepting the reality of the destruction of the Temple, while still looking for its eventual re-establishment by God at some future, Messianic, time. Meanwhile, Christianity was also growing, and separating itself from Judaism, to become a religious movement eventually remote from the Temple cult. Although in the early chapters of Acts the first Christian community apparently worshipped in the Temple, the story of Stephen (Acts 6–7) seems to signal a shift in which the theological rationale of the Temple is increasingly challenged. Christians followed a Lord who had foretold the ruin of the man-made building, to be replaced by the temple of his body. When Christian control was established over Jerusalem in the fourth century AD in the reign of Constantine, the spiritual heart of the city was the Church of the Resurrection (the Holy Sepulchre), the place where that new temple had been raised into life by God. The Temple Mount, by contrast, was deliberately left desolate until the Muslim conquest of Jerusalem; it then became the site of a new sanctuary, *al-Haram al-Sharif*, witnessing to the importance of Jerusalem for the Muslim faith and dramatically asserting the completion and supersession of both Judaism and Christianity by Islam. During the Crusader period, Christian churches were briefly established on the mount, but since the Muslim recapture of the city it has remained an Islamic sanctuary, reckoned to be the third holiest after Mecca and Medina. For most Orthodox Jews, the Temple Mount is a place where access is not permitted as a result of its sanctity.

7.33   How has Jerusalem featured in Zionism? Heartfelt longing for the city continued as a strong theme in diaspora Judaism, expressed perhaps most poignantly in the odes of Judah ha-Levi (c. 1075–1141), which were incorporated in the Jewish liturgy of the Ninth of Av, the commemoration of the destruction of the Temple:

> O Zion, will you not ask how your captives are, the exiles who seek your welfare, who are the remnant of your flock. From west and east, north and south, from every side, accept the greetings of those far and near, and the blessings of this captive of desire, who sheds his tears like the dew of Hermon and longs to have them fall upon your hills. I am like a jackal when I weep for your affliction; but when I dream of your exiles' return, I am a lute for your songs.

There were always devout Jews who followed Judah's example and travelled to the Holy Land for *aliyah*.[86] However, despite the name of the movement, Jerusalem did not have a high profile in the early Jewish Zionist movement, which was essentially agriculturally focused, in a move away from the urban life of the *galut*. The focus of the Israeli pioneers' life was in any case Tel Aviv, not Jerusalem.[87] Yet the echoes of ongoing Jewish longing for Jerusalem can be heard in the Hebrew song *yerushalayim shel zahav* (Jerusalem of Gold). First sung in May 1967, initially before the capture of East Jerusalem by Israeli forces in June of that year, it seemed to act as a precursor for the increasingly high profile Jerusalem would gain in religious Zionism in the later twentieth century. The Temple Mount, in particular the area of the Western Wall, became a focal point in Israeli life after 1967.

7.34   In Christian Zionism, Jerusalem has always featured prominently; and, unlike in traditional Christianity, there is great interest in the Temple Mount. Dispensationalism sees a double role for Jerusalem: now, as the city chosen to be the eternal Jewish capital of Israel; and at the end of time, as the stage for the apocalyptic *dénouement* of history. The two are linked in that the return of the Jews to Jerusalem to greet the Messiah is a necessary step to bring about the millennium. The city's primary importance, on this view, does not come from its being the site of Jesus' death and resurrection. Of still less significance are the historic Christian communities who live there today; if their presence is even acknowledged, they are seen as at best an irrelevance. As to Muslim narratives, these are seen to have no place at all in the story of Jerusalem, and Muslim communities have no right of belonging; the Islamic presence on the Temple Mount in particular is seen as an alien incursion. On the other hand, proposals to rebuild the Temple are enthusiastically supported. Such proposals are seen as a theological necessity and as something that must happen in fulfilment of prophecy.

7.35   An Anglican account of Jerusalem will differ markedly from attitudes of this kind and equally from the view that the city is divested of all spiritual significance since the time of Christ. Three points in particular can be made, again drawing on the theology of *Generous Love*. First, believing that God is creator of all things and Father of all people, Anglicans have an instinct for comprehensiveness which seeks to make space for differing stories to be heard and differing groups to coexist. To some extent this is modelled in the life of the Jerusalem Anglican community itself, which has known significant differences in its composition, and in its mission and pastoral priorities, over its 170 years of history. Today it includes both Arabic and Hebrew speaking congregations, at St George's and at Christ Church respectively. Each has a very different story to tell, and each includes Christians from very different backgrounds and with very different attitudes to the political and social challenges facing the city. This coexistence gives evidence of an instinct to comprehensiveness, however difficult that is to live out in practice. Throughout the city, space must be provided for all communities to live together in harmony and to work together to accommodate their differences peacefully and respectfully.

7.36   Second, the God who invested with universal significance the particular human life of Jesus the Son of God is always and only to be encountered in the specificity of given historical and geographical situations. Places and times matter, and Jerusalem, the city as it has been and as it is, matters more than anywhere else because of Jesus. We cannot accept any account that discounts this reality to make of the city just a stage to act out an apocalyptic drama. Nor can we be content with a spiritualisation that denies any significance to this particular city because the holy is now universally available. Anglicans are suspicious of systematising and totalising approaches, and regard the actual history and current circumstances of the city and of their presence there as important in the shaping of our theology. That history and those circumstances are complicated but unavoidable. We cannot ignore the fact that the Anglican community in Jerusalem began with an attempt to reach out to Jewish people. Even less can we ignore the fact that the community is now primarily Palestinian. Through the voice of our Anglican brothers and sisters, and out of their experiences of marginalisation, occupation, dislocation and dispossession, the voice of Christ speaks specifically to us today.

7.37   Third, in Anglican thinking, the Spirit creates the linkage between the transformation of our inwardness and the flourishing of our life in community; society is the context in which spirituality is expressed. No adequate account of Jerusalem can be given that does not recognise it as an environment for people to live today. Even in a situation as difficult and contested as that of Jerusalem, we need to hold on to the vision of a city where human communities can belong together with respect and understanding in the face of severe strains; and we believe that Christians have a vocation to model such a way of living. We are encouraged by the Bible both to 'pray for the peace of Jerusalem', that its citizens may live together in harmony, and to look for the 'new Jerusalem'. At the centre of the new Jerusalem stands the tree whose leaves are for the healing of the nations, but there is no temple. While we affirm strongly the importance of the holy city, we believe that there is no continuing place in Christian theology for a physical temple.

7.38   The newness of the new Jerusalem is described in Greek not as *nea* but as *kaine*. That implies, not something unconnected with that which has gone before, but rather the renewal of an existing reality. There is to be both continuity and distinction between the current and the new, between the earthly and the heavenly, between Jerusalem as present reality and Jerusalem as future aspiration. Holding together what Dr Rowan Williams, the former Archbishop of Canterbury, has called these two 'overlapping realities' is the challenge we face. It seems to us that the language of 'sacrament' might be used analogically to describe the way in which the city brings these realities together, for the sacramental principle expresses the meeting of the stuff of human experience in this world with the glory of divine life in the world to come. In its human reality, Jerusalem expresses humanity in a double sense. It calls forth the best of our aspirations – it is a place of beauty, a city where people fervently desire to learn, to serve, to worship, to love God. At the same time, it also reveals the worst of our nature – our possessiveness, our divisions, our mistrust, our hatred. In some way, these two are different sides of the same coin, for Jerusalem 'does not simply unveil realities about the human condition, but it also challenges us to address them – truly to become the human beings God created us to be, in God's image and likeness, as God's partners in the creation and repairing of our world'.[88]

7.39   Contemporary theology speaks of the sacraments in terms of sign, of instrument, and of foretaste. As sign, a sacrament needs a solid physical reality to serve as a vehicle of the divine presence; we believe that created realities are not abolished through serving as points of encounter with God. Thus to speak of Jerusalem as sacramental is not to appropriate it to the Church in a way that evacuates it of its many-layered complexity. Jerusalem is at one and the same time Jewish, Christian, Muslim and secular, at one and the same time, Israeli, Palestinian and international. The reality of the city will always resist any reduction of itself to a piece of Christian symbolism; it will always – this side of the eschaton – be a place of incompletion, brokenness, untidiness. Yet Jerusalem understood as sacrament is also an instrument for the divine purpose of salvation. The city is not only a human project, trying to provide a place for the God whom no human house can hold; it is also God's own project, the place from which he reached out and continues to reach out to humanity, in the Temple, in the Christ, in the Spirit-filled community of today. And a sacramental vision of Jerusalem recognises it as foretaste: it must hold out to those in hopelessness the hope of God's coming justice. So we have heard, and we wish to affirm, the words of the *Kairos Palestine* statement endorsed by the churches of Jerusalem:

Jerusalem is the foundation of our vision and our entire life. She is the city to which God gave a particular importance in the history of humanity. She is the city to which all people are in movement – and where they will meet in friendship and love in the presence of the one unique God, according to the vision of the prophet Isaiah:

> *In days to come the mountain of the Lord's house shall be established as*
> *the highest of the mountains, and shall be raised above the hills;*
> *all the nations shall stream to it.*[89]

Chapter 8

Mapping our views

8.1   We came to the task of writing this report as a group of Anglicans of quite diverse views, and recognising that we were dealing with issues about which there is not merely diversity but passionately conducted disagreements among Anglicans, as among other Christians. We are also very conscious that, like the overwhelming majority of Christians worldwide, although we are bound to the Holy Land by strong bonds of interest and affection, Israel and Palestine are not our countries. That means we do not have to live with the daily realities faced by Christians, Jews, Muslims and others who live in the Holy Land; and that in turn lays on us not only a responsibility to listen to those who do live there, but also a responsibility to be thoughtful and careful in the language we use and the actions we take, because we do not have to live directly with the consequences. That said, we have come to three conclusions: that there are some key principles on which we agree, and which we believe are consonant with our understanding of the Anglican theological insights set out in this document (especially in chapter 5); that there are some beliefs and attitudes which we cannot accept, and which we believe do not accord with our understanding of Anglican theological insights; and that there are some issues on which we sincerely hold different views, and on which we think vigorous but courteous debate needs to continue among Anglicans.

In the lists of beliefs and attitudes set out below, the references given in brackets relate to the paragraph(s) in the report which discuss or substantiate the assertions we are making. The references are indicative, and not necessarily exhaustive.

8.2   **We wish to affirm the following:**

- God is equally concerned for all peoples and all lands *(5.3; 7.29; 7.35)*

- Our primary identity is given in Jesus Christ, and this must be prior to our national or ethnic identity *(7.20)*

- All Christians are of equal standing in the Church, whether Jewish or 'Gentile', indigenous or migrant *(7.18)*

- God has acted decisively at specific times in history in the Holy Land, supremely in the life, death and resurrection of Jesus of Nazareth *(5.3; 5.9; 7.30-1; 7.36)*

- All scripture is inspired by God, and needs interpretation in the light of Jesus Christ *(5.5; 7.28)*

- The spiritual and the material have to be held together, as do the particular and the universal *(5.12; 7.2; 7.4-8)*

- It is essential to sustain a Christian, and in particular an Anglican, presence in the Holy Land *(Foreword; 5.7; 5.11-12; 7.1; 7.9)*

- It is essential to sustain a Christian, and in particular an Anglican, presence in Jerusalem *(Foreword; 5.7; 5.11-12; 7.1; 7.9; 7.36)*

- Christians around the world have a duty to pray for, listen to and be in solidarity with their fellow Christians in the Holy Land *(Foreword; 7.1)*

- Anglicans around the world have a duty to pray for, listen to and be in solidarity with their fellow Anglicans in the Holy Land *(Foreword; 7.1; 7.36)*

- The particular place which the land of Israel and city of Jerusalem hold for Jewish people must be taken seriously by Christians *(2.6; 2.15; 7.11)*

- The figure of Israel speaks to us all of the way we have to struggle with the Word of God *(1.1-3)*

- Israel as a people has been chosen by God to serve his mission *(1.1-3)*

- The Jewish people have a continuing role within the purposes of God *(6.52; Afterword)*

- The advances made in Jewish-Christian relations over the last fifty years must be consolidated and developed *(5.1; 6.34; 6.36; 6.42; Afterword)*

- All who live in the Holy Land should have equal access to land, water, and other resources, and an equal guarantee of security *(2.31-32; 7.16-17)*

- Legitimate concerns about security must not be used by any party as an excuse unilaterally to alter boundaries without the consent of other affected parties *(2.28; 7.17; Afterword)*

- Jewish, Christian and Muslim people should have equal freedom to practise their religions in the Holy Land and in Jerusalem, as these are holy to all their faiths *(2.30; 6.6; 7.32-33; 7.39)*

- There must be dialogue concerning the Holy Land and Jerusalem which involves Christians, Jews and Muslims *(5.7; 7.10)*

- The State of Israel is an established national state, and its citizens have the right to live in security, peace and freedom *(2.33; 2.36; 6.37; 7.17)*

- Palestine has a national identity, with a cultural heritage to be acknowledged and respected; Palestinians in the West Bank and Gaza have the right to live in freedom, peace and security without military occupation or appropriation of land, and to self-determination. *(2.36; 7.17)*

- Christians should seek the resolution of conflict, the understanding and meeting of the needs of all concerned, and international cooperation without prejudice *(2.40; 5.3; 5.7; 6.51-52; 7.29)*

- Human rights must be observed by all jurisdictions in the Holy Land *(7.15)*

- There should be no limits to our expressions of neighbourliness on the basis of religion, ethnicity or nationality *(5.3; 6.43; 7.12; 7.16-17)*

- Peace and justice cannot be divorced *(2.22; 6.49; 6.51; 7.29)*

8.3 **We consider that the following beliefs and attitudes are unacceptable within the boundaries of an Anglican interpretation of Christian faith:**

- God has given the Holy Land as an exclusive possession to any one community *(4.1; 5.3; 7.10-18)*

- God has given Jerusalem as an exclusive possession to any one community *(7.35-39)*

- Jews have forfeited any right to live in the Holy Land because of their alleged disobedience *(7.5; 7.10-18)*

- Christians, Muslims and others have no right to live in the Holy Land because it has been given by God to the Jews *(4.1)*

- God has no interest in human history, and his workings cannot be discerned there *(5.9-10; 7.25-26)*

- Prophecy as prediction can be separated from prophecy as ethics *(5.6; 7.14; 7.29)*

- The interpretation of scripture can lead to a clear timetable of the end times *(5.6; 7.27-29)*

- The physical re-establishment of the Temple in Jerusalem is a goal which Christians should seek *(7.34-35)*

- It is ever right to think, speak or act with hatred towards others *(7.29)*

- The door to reconciliation is ever closed *(7.29; 7.37)*

- Violence or terrorism is a way of serving God *(5.6; 7.29)*

- We should give up on hope, or relish the prospect of destruction *(5.6)*

8.4 **We recognise that there are significantly different views on a number of issues held with integrity among those who hold to an Anglican interpretation of the Christian faith – including the following:**

- The theological significance of Israel as a partner in a continuing covenant with God *(2.17)*

- The significance of the events of 1948 and 1967, in the light of prophecy and of God's providential care *(2.8; 7.23-25)*

- The status of Israel as a Jewish state *(2.9; 2.18)*

- The moral duty of Christians to support the State of Israel in light of the history of anti-Judaism and the Holocaust *(2.16)*

- The call to direct action for Palestinian advocacy as an overriding imperative for Christians *(2.35; 2.37)*

- Ways to acknowledge and safeguard Jerusalem's status as a Holy City for Judaism, Christianity and Islam *(7.30; 7.32-33; 7.39)*

- The detailed structures of governance and security which will best enable lasting peace and justice in the Holy Land *(2.36)*

8.5 These are issues which require us to listen carefully to the voices of those who live in Israel and Palestine – people of every community, but especially our Anglican and other Christian brothers and sisters – and to listen carefully to one another, especially to those with whom we disagree. We are to listen not merely as if we were dealing with a human and political situation that is particularly complex and apparently intractable (though we are) but also as people seeking the will of the God who has made himself definitively known in this particular situation. As we recognise that debate will continue, and seek to contribute to that debate, we recognise above all that this is a situation for which we are called to pray, in the words of the Psalmist:

> Pray for the peace of Jerusalem;
>> may they prosper who love you.
> Peace be within your walls
>> and prosperity within your palaces.
> For my kindred and companions' sake
>> I will pray that peace be with you.
> For the sake of the house of the Lord our God
>> I will seek to do you good.
>
> *(Psalm 122.6-8)*

Afterword
The Most Revd Dr Rowan Williams, former Archbishop of Canterbury

It's strange to think that *Zion* – once a word full of hope and imaginative excitement for Christians and Jews alike – has become so wrapped up in controversy. For so many centuries it was a symbol of the homecoming that all the children of Abraham long for, a symbol of reconciled and healed belonging together: 'They stand those halls of Sion/Conjubilant with song'; 'Saviour, since of Zion's city/ I through grace a member am…'; and so on. But 'Zionism' has become a code word: once itself expressing hope for a scattered, abused community, it is now for many a trigger for fear and suspicion. It is included in catalogues of unacceptable ideologies. In the rhetoric of a large part of the world, especially the Muslim world, it stands for something aggressive and unreconciled. Yet to be 'against' Zionism is so readily interpreted as being hostile to the very heart of Jewish identity as many understand it. What is a Christian, an Anglican Christian in particular, to make of the phenomenon of Zionism, and in particular the various forms of Christian Zionism?

The foregoing pages represent a deeply careful and sensitive attempt to answer this – sometimes agonised – question. We have seen here a painstaking mapping of the various ways in which the language of 'Zionist' aspiration has been expressed and the various ways in which it has been taken on board by Christians. We have been guided through some of the history of the Jewish people's relations with English Christians, and the complex story of twentieth century developments. We have been pointed to aspects of our Anglican tradition that may help us in reading the record of scriptural promises and in at least beginning to see what it means to invest a specific territory with the meanings of God himself – and to see the risks of doing this in abstraction from a clear sense of God's own universal hospitality. This report will not sit comfortably with those who see no argument about the issues involved in the Holy Land today, those for whom the basic questions are crystal clear. But we must hope that it will assist those who share an honest perplexity.

Some things are clear. It is clear that no Christian can for a moment entertain the possibility that the Jewish people should ever again find themselves at the mercy of a genocidally hostile environment, with no home to call their own and no resources to defend themselves. The State of Israel must be a place where there can never be any doubt that Jewish people are welcome and safe. But it is clear also that the maintenance of such safety at the cost of justice for others, at the cost of a perpetually anxious and militarised culture that cannot find room for the rights and dignities of neighbours, is a real danger to just that welcome and the safety that the State of Israel seeks to guarantee. Israel has been at the receiving end of appalling aggression and random violence. But this history does not move out of the tragic cycle of bitterness and revenge if the response is one that sows the seeds of more furious resentment. This report rightly asks the fundamental question of what will be lastingly just for everyone.

Thus it is critical of that strange modern style of Christian rhetoric which brushes aside any moral challenge to the State of Israel's behaviour, any appeal to a biblical ethic of justice or hospitality in this regard, any consideration of the dignities and rights of Palestinians and others in the Holy Land and the occupied territories, any compassion for the innocent who suffer in this setting – and , most oddly of all, any attention to the needs of the long-established Christian communities of the Holy Land. To be serious about the ongoing vocation of the Jewish people in God's purpose and about the legitimacy of the State of Israel and its need to be free from assault and the threat of terror does not mean asking no questions or ignoring the plight of those who are most obviously humiliated and disadvantaged by present policies. It is absolutely true that in order to ask awkward questions in an effective way we need to become trusted friends; and equally true that our history as Christians gives little encouragement to our Jewish neighbours to think that we could ever really be such. But if it is hard to be a truly critical friend, this does not mean that critical friendship is any less essential.

Perhaps one of the most useful elements in these pages has been the lucid summary of what we may expect to hold in common as Anglicans in respect of these matters and what we are likely to disagree about. As the report's conclusion says, we are committed to a painful and demanding listening to those who are most directly affected. The old Jewish saying about Jerusalem being the crucible for the 'testing of hearts' is sharply applicable. Our hope and prayer must be that the reflections offered here will likewise be for the testing of hearts, for the refining of our sympathies and our aspirations. Can 'Zion' be heard once again as a word that evokes a universal citizenship, a home for the homeless, the passionate faithfulness of God to his promise to make his Name dwell among us? The issues of justice for all in the Holy Land should hold those questions unsparingly before us.

Endnotes

1   See rowanwilliams.archbishopofcanterbury.org, and enter 'Easter sermon 2012' in the Search box

2   Clare Amos, *The Book of Genesis*, Epworth Press, Peterborough, 2004, p.228

3   wikipedia.org/wiki/Zionism

4   www.zionism-israel.com/zionism_definitions.htm

5   Victoria Clark, Allies for Armageddon: The Rise of Christian Zionism, New Haven: Yale University Press, 2007

6   www.jewsnotzionists.org/differencejudzion.html

7   www.informationclearinghouse.info/article4549.htm

8   www.yachadblog.org.uk/2012/04/liberation-occupy-zionism/

9   en.wikipedia.org/wiki/Christian_Zionism

10   www.christianzionism.org/Article/Wagner02.asp

11   www.zionismontheweb.org/christian_zionism/

12   Clark, Allies for Armageddon, pp.3,6

13   In the Old Testament, particularly in poetic books such as the Psalms, 'Zion' is regularly used as a synonym of 'Jerusalem'

14   Robert O. Smith, 'Anglo-American Christian Zionism: Implications for Palestinian Christians', *The Ecumenical Review* 64.1, March 2012, p.28

15   The King James Version translates this verse as including an instruction by Paul to Timothy to 'rightly divide the word of truth' i.e. 'divide up' the past and future referred to in the Bible into several eras or 'dispensations'

16   The history of dispensationalism is discussed in more detail at chapter 6.17-18. See also Stephen Sizer, *Christian Zionism: Road-map to Armageddon?*, Nottingham: IVP, 2004. Sizer's book focuses specifically on pre-millennial dispensationalist forms of Christian Zionism.

17   One suggested list of the core beliefs of Christian Zionism is given by the Anglican Palestinian priest Naim Ateek as follows:

     • Christian Zionists cling to a literal belief in an inerrant and infallible Bible.

     • All biblical prophecies must be fulfilled literally.

     • The Jewish people are God's chosen people.

- The land of Palestine is Eretz Yisrael (the land of Israel) and has been given by God to Jews exclusively as an eternal inheritance.

- Jews must return to Palestine in fulfilment of biblical prophecies and establish their state (their kingdom).

- Jerusalem belongs exclusively to the Jewish people.

- The Jewish Temple must be rebuilt in order to usher in the second coming of Christ.

- The Rapture will remove Christian believers from the earth so they will avoid and escape the Great Tribulation.

- The great battle of Armageddon will take place at the end of history when two-thirds of the Jewish people will be killed and the last third will accept Jesus as the true messiah.

- Jesus will return to earth and reign for a thousand years. Then the forces of evil will rise up again and will be totally exterminated by Christ. A new heaven and a new earth will come into being and God's kingdom of righteousness will be established forever. The Jews will reign in their kingdom on earth and Christians will reign in their kingdom in heaven.

(Naim Stifan Ateek, *A Palestinian Christian Cry for Reconciliation*, Maryknoll: Orbis: 2008 p.82)

18   National Jewish Scholars Project 15.07.2002, *Dabru Emet: A Jewish Statement on Christians and Christianity*, at www.jcrelations.net, then follow links to Statements - Jewish

19   For example, the mission organisation CMJ (the Church's Ministry Among the Jewish people) states 'CMJ believes that the term "Restoration" when applied to the Jewish people is primarily restoration to their Messiah, Yeshua HaMashiach, Jesus the Christ; and secondarily restoration to a safe homeland after 2000 years of persecution.'

20   Although there are reports from a range of sources that an uprising was planned that year, the flashpoint for the Intifada is generally given as a provocative walk of Israeli opposition leader Ariel Sharon on the *al-Haram al-Sharif*,/Temple Mount.

21   The Israeli Human Rights organisation, B'Tselem, publishes regular reports. Its March 2012 report, 'Under the Guise of Legality', can be found by visiting www.btselem.org, putting 'legality' into the search box; select the item entitled 'BTselem Report: Under the guise of legality'

22   B'Tselem report on the number and nature of check-points and other restrictions: www.btselem.org/freedom_of_movement/checkpoints

23   Regarding the lack of Palestinian confidence in the Israeli legal system, see the Palestinian Centre for Human Rights' Submission to the UN Committee on the Elimination of Racial Discrimination in February 2012:
www2.ohchr.org/english/bodies/cerd/docs/ngos/PCHR_Israel_CERD80.pdf
The legal department of Rabbis for Human Rights supports claims through Israeli courts: rhr.org.il/eng/index.php/about-legal-department-2/

24   The UN's Relief and Works Agency is the most visible sign of support within Gaza supplying humanitarian aid: www.unrwa.org/palestine-refugees

25   Wikipedia and other sources annotate the results: Final results show that Hamas won the election, with 74 seats to the ruling Fatah's 45, providing Hamas with the majority of the 132 available

seats and the ability to form a majority government on their own. Of the Electoral Lists, Hamas received 44.45 percent and Fatah 41.43 percent and of the Electoral Districts, Hamas party candidates received 41.73 percent and Fatah party candidates received 36.96 percent.

26   Figures for casualties are disputed, but more than 1300 Gazans were killed, with around 13 Israel Defense Force deaths and over 30 serious injuries (information agreed by a range of sources)

27   See Wallerstein & Silverman's report of March 2009:
      eng.bimkom.org/_Uploads/28Housingdistressjaffa.pdf

      Recent visits by the authors in 2010 and 2011 suggest that little has changed.

28   See statistics and reports by B'Tselem, Ir Amim and Rabbis for Human Rights et al. Also see reports on the organisation 'Elad', redeveloping Silwan, including at:
      peacenow.org/entries/wp264 and apjp.org/silwan/

29   See, e.g.: news.bbc.co.uk/2/hi/8366596.stm

30   www.kairospalestine.ps/

31   Operative Paragraph One, 'Affirms that the fulfillment of Charter principles requires the establishment of a just and lasting peace in the Middle East which should include the application of both the following principles:

      (i) Withdrawal of Israel armed forces from territories occupied in the recent conflict;

      (ii) Termination of all claims or states of belligerency and respect for and acknowledgment of the sovereignty, territorial integrity and political independence of every State in the area and their right to live in peace within secure and recognized boundaries free from threats or acts of force.'

32   As noted elsewhere, this allows anyone with a Jewish grandparent to apply for residency in Israel.

33   Motion GS 1874B. For a briefing paper prepared by Mission and Public Affairs Council, Public Affairs Council, visit www.churchofengland.org', search for 'Motion GS 1874B' and select the Word document entitled 'GS 1874B

34   See rowanwilliams.archbishopofcanterbury.org; search for 'July 2011' and click on 'Conference on Christians in the Holy Land - opening speeches'

35   Martin Buber, '*The Land and its Possessors*', in *Israel and the World: Essays in a Time of Crisis*, New York: Schocken Books, 1948, pp.227–233 (extracts)

36   Naim Ateek, 'Biblical perspectives on the Land', in *Faith and the Intifada*, ed. Naim Ateek, Marc H. Ellis, Rosemary Radford Ruether, Maryknoll NY: Orbis, 1992, p.108.

37   Naim Stifan Ateek, *A Palestinian Christian Cry for Reconciliation*, Maryknoll NY: Orbis, 2008, pp.53–54.

38   CMJ Israel has produced a statement on 'Israel and the Palestinians': visit www.cjj-israel.org, and find the link on the 'About CMJ' page

39   www.cmj.org.uk/about/cmjzionist

40   www.iccj.org/fileadmin/ICCJ/pdf-Dateien/A_Time_for_Recommitment_engl.pdf

41   www.kairospalestine.ps/sites/default/Documents/English.pdf

42   David Rosen, 'Zionism: the perspective of a religious peacenik', *Common Ground*, Summer 2011, p.10–11

43   The story is based on information given in Keith Carley, 'Psalms for Worship, An Assessment', *Journeyings*, November 1989, pp.31–32

44   The 1897 Lambeth Conference had passed two resolutions concerning Jews and Muslims, but these could not be described as dialogical

45   Network for Interfaith Concerns of the Anglican Communion, *Generous Love: the truth of the Gospel and the call to dialogue*, Anglican Consultative Council, 2008

46   It is notable that during the Reformation and the compilation of the lectionary linked now to the Book of Common Prayer Archbishop Cranmer discouraged over interest in the Book of Revelation – a favourite biblical book of Christian Zionism

47   See Rowan Williams, *Anglican Identities*, London: DLT, 2004

48   'The Catechism', *1662 Book of Common Prayer*

49   'Article XXVIII: Of The Lord's Supper', *Articles of Religion, Book of Common Prayer*

50   See 2.14. 'Restorationism' (i.e. belief in the 'restoration' of the Jewish people to Jerusalem etc.) is the formally correct term to use in relation to the seventeenth century as the terms Zionism and Christian Zionism did not come into use until later in history.

51   The London Society was the forerunner of the current CMJ, the Church's Ministry among Jewish People, formerly called the Church's Mission to the Jews

52   An outline of dispensationalist thinking is to be found in the notes on the text in *The Schofield Reference Bible* (1917 edition), pub. Oxford University Press

53   CMS more recently changed its name (though not its initials) to 'Church Mission Society'

54   Numbers vary. The Prussian Consul Dr Schulze recorded a Jerusalem population of 16,410, including 7,120 Jews, in 1845. Revd F.C. Ewald wrote in 1843 about continuing immigration, mentioning 150 Jews recently arrived from Algeria (Gilbert, M. 2008, *The Routledge Historical Atlas of Jerusalem*, 4th edition)

55   On this, see Johnson, P. *A History of the Jews*, pub. London: George Weidenfeld &Nicholson, 1987, especially p.377

56   According to a Midrash in the Talmud, God required two oaths of the Jewish people and one of the Gentiles: Jews were not to go from exile to the Land as a body, neither were they to rebel against the other nations. For their part, Gentiles were abjured to treat the Jews fairly.

57   Quotation from official letter from the UK Foreign Office 14 August, 1903 by Clement Hill (writing on behalf of the Marquis of Lansdowne) to L. J. Greenberg in regard to 'the form of an agreement which Dr Herzl proposes should be entered into between His Majesty's government and the Jewish Colonial Trust, Ltd., for the establishment of a Jewish settlement in East Africa.'

58   Ronald Sanders, *The High Walls of Jerusalem: History of the Balfour Declaration and the Birth of the British Mandate for Palestine*, New York: Holt Rinehart & Winston, 1984, p. 315 ff

59   Complete text of the Balfour Declaration available at http://unispal.un.og: enter 'Balfour' in the Search box

60 The Nazi definition of 'Who is a Jew?' and thus a target for persecution and eventual extermination was primarily a racial/ethnic, rather than religious one. People were considered to be Jewish if they had one Jewish grandparent, even if they did not themselves profess the Jewish faith, and even if they had converted to another faith, such as Christianity.

61 In 1941, during the war, Hitler and the Nazi leadership was visited by the Grand Mufti Haj Amin al-Husseini, who saw the Nazis as sharing 'natural enemies': Jews, British and communists. www.worldfuturefund.org/wffmaster/Reading/Total/hitler.mufti.htm; et al.

62 A leading figure in the Irgun was Menachem Begin, later Prime Minister of Israel

63 United Nations Resolution 181 (ii) Palestine; see www.un.org and for related Security Council resolutions in 1947/8.

64 *United Nations Special Committee on Palestine* (UNSCOP) report, 1947

65 For Plan Dalet, the final phase of this strategy, see:
www.jewishvirtuallibrary.org/jsource/History/Plan_Dalet.html

66 For a personal, Christian account of these events, see: Chacour, E. *Blood Brothers*, Lincoln, Virginia: Chosen Books, 1984

67 See www.un.org/en/sc/documents/resolutions; click on 1967 to find Resolution 242

68 UN S A Framework for peace between Israel and Egypt, brokered by US President Jimmy Carter, was agreed between Anwar al-Sadat and Menachim Begin on 17 September 1978. Although some of the five-year plan was implemented, not all the terms were satisfactorily concluded. Both Begin and Sadat were joint recipients of the Nobel Peace Prize in 1978.

69 See chapter 3.3 for extracts from the writings of Naim Ateek

70 Information about Sabeel, which has now developed a number of international support groups, can be found at www.sabeel.org

71 United Nations Security Council resolution 446, adopted on 22 March 1979, stated: 'that the policy and practices of Israel in establishing settlements in the Palestinian and other Arab territories occupied since 1967 have no legal validity and constitute a serious obstruction to achieving a comprehensive, just and lasting peace in the Middle East'.

72 *The Alexandria Declaration:*
http://nifcon.anglicancommunion.org/work/declarations/alexandria.cfm

73 The text of *The Way of Dialogue* is accessible online at
www.anglicancommunion.org/the-holy-land/info/lambeth1.cfm

74 *Sharing One Hope? The Church of England and Christian-Jewish Relations;* London: Church House Publishing, 2001, p.16. See www.aco.org/the-holy-land/data/Sharing.pdf

75 nifcon.anglicancommunion.org/work/dialogues/ajc/index.cfm

76 nifcon.anglicancommunion.org/work/dialogues/al_ahzar/index.cfm

77 Archbishop of Canterbury's opening remarks at the International Conference on Christians in the Holy Land held at Lambeth Palace, July 2011. See n.34

78   John Hagee, *Final Dawn over Jerusalem*, Nashville: Thomas Nelson, 2000, p. 19, quoted in Colin Chapman, *Whose Holy City? Jerusalem and the Israeli-Palestinian Conflict*, Oxford: Lion Publishing, 2004, p.122

79   Norman C. Habel, *The Land is Mine: Six Biblical Land Ideologies*, Fortress: Minneapolis, 1995, p.146

80   See extract from Buber's writings, chapter 3.2

81   In later (and contemporary) Jewish usage, the *gērīm* are understood to be those from a Gentile background who, by taking observance of the Torah upon themselves, have identified themselves as members of the people of Israel, i.e. proselytes

82   The Hebrew Bible is known as the *Tanakh* because of the order in which its books are arranged. While the order of the Greek Septuagint (followed by the Christian Old Testament) is: (1) Law, (2) Writings (including all the historical books), (3) Prophets, the *Tanakh* is an acronym for the Hebrew order: (1) Law (*Torah*), (2) Prophets (*Nevi'im* – in which are included 1 and 2 Samuel and 1 and 2 Kings), (3) Writings (*Kethuvim*). The last book of the Bible in the *Tanakh* sequence is 2 Chronicles.

83   Verse 6 of the hymn *O quanta qualia sunt illa Sabbata* (Peter Abelard, 1079-1142), tr. J.M.Neale as 'O what their joy and their glory must be', *English Hymnal* no. 465

84   Fawzi al-Asmar, 'I shall not despair', *The Wind-driven Reed*, tr. From the Arabic by Fawzi al-Asmar, G. Kanazeh and Uri Davis, Washington D.C.: Three Continents Press, 1979, quoted in Kenneth Cragg, *This Year in Jerusalem: Israel in Experience*, London; Darton, Longman and Todd, 1982, p.86

85   'Article VII: Of the Old Testament', *Articles of Religion, Book of Common Prayer*

86   *Aliyah*, from the Hebrew verb 'to go up', is the term used at least since the late nineteenth century to describe Jewish immigration to the Holy Land

87   Moreover, within the Jerusalem area itself, secular Zionists sought to develop Mount Herzl as an alternative focus to the ancient religious holy sites - in some paradoxical sense, it could be said, a Zionist replacement for Zion

88   Clare Amos, *O Jerusalem*, unpublished paper delivered at the Anglican-Jewish Dialogue Commission, 2009

89   *Kairos Palestine document: A Moment of Truth*, 9.5